Contents

Mary Cawkell

The Falkland Story
1592 — 1982

Anthony Nelson

024278

First published in 1983 by Anthony Nelson,
P.O. Box 9, Oswestry, Shropshire SY11 1BY England

ISBN 0 904614 08 5

Printed in Great Britain by Livesey Limited, Shrewsbury, England.

Foreword

Mary Cawkell is the historian of the Falkland Islands. When her book *The Falklands Islands* was published in 1960 it immediately became the standard modern history of the discovery, exploration and settlement of the Islands, replacing the book of the same name written by Miss Boyson forty years earlier. In her first book Mary Cawkell demolished many of the inaccuracies in Julius Goebel's thesis work *The Struggle for the Falklands* published in the United States in 1927.

How thoroughly Mary Cawkell had researched her subject may be seen from the bibliography appended to her first book on the Islands, which occupies thirteen pages. How insignificant in practical terms the Argentine claim to sovereignty over the Islands was in 1960 may be judged from the fact that "Argentina" appeared only three times in the Index.

In this shorter work, Mary Cawkell has covered four hundred years of the Islands' story and brought the narrative down to the Argentine invasion on 2nd April 1982. She was a witness to many of the events of the nineteen fifties when she lived in the Islands and was Honorary Secretary of the Broadcasting Committee and a pioneer of further education. She has remained in close touch with events ever since.

The Argentine version of the history of the claim to sovereignty has gone around the world with the full resources of the Argentine Government behind it. This book supplies the corrective.

Mary Cawkell has a historian's passion for accuracy and she writes with a passionate belief in the Islands and their sturdy people. She spares no one as she tells the dismal story of British Governmental incompetence and exploitation by individuals over the last century and a half which has led to the neglect of a land of great potential and even greater strategic importance.

Almost the first event in each world war was a battle by British fleets based in the Islands for control of the South Atlantic — Coronel and the Battle of the Falkland Islands in 1914 and the Battle of the River Plate in 1939. Mary Cawkell has chronicled the neglect and mishandling in time of peace which encouraged the Argentine Government to believe we did not care. If the lessons are learnt, perhaps a nation can still be built in the Falkland Islands.

E. W. Hunter Christie.

Preface

Since the publication of my earlier, detailed history, I have continued my study of the Falkland Islands. This book, based largely on the additional material I have acquired since 1960, aims to present in a concise, summarised form the complete story of the Falklands from their discovery up to 2 April 1982, when the Argentine forces invaded.

It does not concern itself with political argument. Events are seen and, where necessary, interpreted in the circumstances of their occurring.

If the book has a purpose it is to elucidate rather than explain, to dispel some of the fog in which the story of the islands, due to their geographical situation — distant from populated lands, seemingly over-close to Antarctica — has become shrouded. The fact that the islands throughout the colonial period were permitted to remain under-populated and unregarded has also helped exacerbate this state of affairs, resulting in what is plain and straightforward acquiring an air of conundrum and mystery.

The last chapter, dealing with the period 1964 to 1982 when the attempt was made artificially to divert the course of the Islands' history, has necessarily had to be given in some detail in order to present a comprehensible picture of the unfolding events and their drift to the inevitable result.

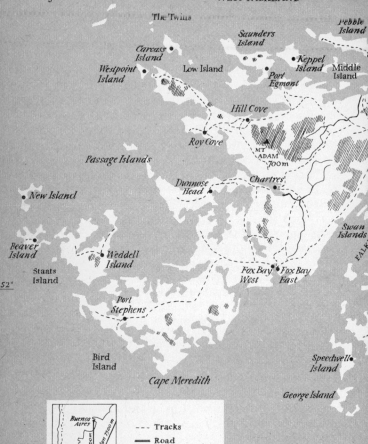

Steeple
Jason   Grand
        Jason

WEST FALKLAND

The Twins

Pebble
Island

Carcass
Island

Saunders
Island

Keppel
Island

Westpoint
Island

Low Island

Port
Egmont

Middle
Island

Hill Cove

Roy Cove

Passage Islands

MT
ADAM
700m

New Island

Dunnose
Head

Chartres

Beaver
Island

Weddell
Island

Swan
Islands

Staats
Island

FALK

Fox Bay
West

Fox Bay
East

52°

Port
Stephens

Bird
Island

Speedwell
Island

Cape Meredith

George Island

Buenos
Aires

London 7500m

1500m

600m

- - - - Tracks
——— Road
  • Settlements

61°   60°

61°   60°

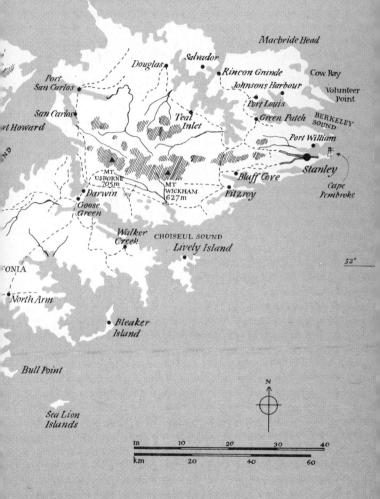

Sources

Argentina, *Statement by the Representative of, H.E. Dr. Jose Maria Ruda,* before Subcommittee III of the Special Committee on the situation with regard to the Implementation of the Declaration on the Granting of Independence to Colonial Countries and People. Malvinas Islands (New York, 9 September 1964.)

Bassett, Marnie, *Realms and Islands. The World Voyage of Rose de Freycinet in the Corvette URANIE 1817-1820* (1962)

Cawkell, M. B. R., Maling, D. M., Cawkell, E. M., *The Falkland Islands* (1960)

Economist Intelligence Unit (Chairman: Lord Shackleton), *Economic Survey of the Falkland Islands, Vols. 1 & 2* (1976)

Falkland Islands Journal, 1968-1981

Falkland Islands Monthly Reviews, October 1964 to November 1973

Falkland Islands Newsletters, November 1977 to June 1981

Falkland Islands Times, December 1973 to December 1981

Falkland News, 26 August 1977

Ferns, H. S., *Britain and Argentina in the 19th Century* (1960)

Ferns, H. S., *Argentina* (1969)

Fitzroy, Captain Robert, R.N., *A Narrative of the Voyage of H.M.S. BEAGLE* (Edited by David Stanbury) (1977)

Friends Of The Falkland Islands Newsletters, March & November 1976, June 1977

Goebel, Julius, Jr., *The Struggle for the Falkland Islands* (1971)

Kirkpatrick, F. A., *A History of the Argentine Republic* (1931)

Overseas Development Administration, *Report on the Sheep and Cattle Industries of the Falkland Islands* (1971)

Parry, J. H., *The Spanish Seaborne Empire* (1966)

Pigafetta, Antonio, *Magellan's Voyage* (Translated by R. A. Skelton) (1975)

Riesenberg, Felix, *Cape Horn* (1950)

The Times Parliamentary Reports, 1968 to 1981

Wannop, A. R., *Report on Visits to Falkland Islands Sheep Stations* (1961).

Chapter 1

Discovery

Disputation over the Falkland Islands began with their discovery. They were discovered on 14 August 1592 by John Davis when his ship, *Desire,* was storm-driven in among them. Davis, second in command of Sir Thomas Cavendish's second expedition into the South Seas, had lost contact with the other ships when the fleet was forced by bad weather in the Strait of Magellan to put back into the South Atlantic. The *Desire* and the pinnace *Black* reached the agreed regrouping point, Port Desire on the Patagonian coast, where Davis had to remain two months carrying out necessary repairs. The *Desire,* a much worn vessel when it joined the expedition — it had been Cavendish's flag-ship when he made his earlier spectacular (second English) navigation of the world — had suffered severely in the Strait and subsequently.

Davis was making his way from Port Desire to the Strait in the hope of finding that Cavendish had returned there when, as John Jane, who travelled on the *Desire* and chronicled the voyage, records:

On the 9th we had a sore storme so that we were constrained to hull, for our sailes were not to indure any force. The 14th we were driven in among certaine isles never before discovered by any known relation, lying fifty leagues or better from the shore east and northerly from the straite, in which place unless it had pleased God of his wonderful mercie to have ceased the winds, we must of necessity have perished.

On 18 August Davis was back in the Strait to begin what was to be a vain search for Cavendish.

Apologists for a Spanish discovery of the islands make much of the fact that English chroniclers of the time, particularly Hakluyt, then engaged on his famous work *The Principal Navigations, Voyages and Discoveries of the*

English Nation, failed to give public recognition to this discovery. Hakluyt knew the merits of Davis as a navigator. He had chronicled his two famous voyages to the Arctic when Davis probed farther north than any voyager thitherto.

He would have been aware of Davis' return voyage from the Strait — a sea epic in its own right — how through every conceivable disaster he had brought the broken *Desire* on its one fluked anchor from the Pacific end of the Strait to the little Irish port of Beerhaven. Davis was also available. He spent the two years after his return, ashore, writing his two books *The Seaman's Secrets* and *The World's Hydrographical Description.*

The reason why immediate recognition was not accorded to Davis' discovery and for its being ignored for some time after was undoubtedly the letter from Cavendish which preceded Davis home.

When Cavendish set out on his second expedition he was a national hero. He had returned from his first voyage a month after the defeat of the Armada when nationalist feelings were running high. The little *Desire,* as it sailed up the Thames, was bedecked in blue damask. In its hold were the contents of the captured Spanish treasure ship. The Queen waved to Cavendish from Greenwich Palace as he sailed by. Later she knighted him.

The second voyage, ill-prepared, fraught with disagreements among the captains of the various vessels — off Brazil one refused to continue and returned to England — and horrendous weather in the Strait, sapped Cavendish's resources and it would seem affected his mind. Instead of making for Port Desire to join Davis, he continued northwards, accompanied by the remaining ship of the expedition which deserted him farther up the Patagonian coast with most of the supplies. Cavendish came to final anchor at Ascension Island where he was to die. Before expiry, he wrote to the executor of his will a scurrilous letter accusing Davis of treachery and of causing the ruin of the expedition. Davis returned home

to find himself a discredited man. Not being one who
sought the limelight — he was the only one of the
Elizabethan navigators not to be knighted — he settled
down to his writing and eventually went back to sea. In
the England of his day a man who captured Spanish
treasure ships was of more significance than one who
only enlarged the prospect of the world. The fact that
Hakluyt was married to Cavendish's sister could well
have played a part in the non-recognition of Davis'
discovery.

There was also at the time much confusion regarding
the islands off the Patagonian coast which Magellan's
voyaging to discover the Strait had revealed, a confusion
arising from the fact that no log of Magellan's voyage
survived and the map-makers of the time had to rely on
word of mouth and memory of the survivors when they
eventually returned to Spain. Placing islands by an
undefined coast-line in an indefinite part of the world
presented the early cartographers with considerable
difficulties. Baffled as to their exact whereabouts, they
placed them in a variety of places between the Plate
estuary and the Strait of Magellan. Some, altogether
baffled, placed them nowhere. Since Magellan had
discovered the islands on the way to the Strait, a favourite
place for putting them was just before he entered the
waterway in a relationship that increasingly became
north-east. From this placing, apologists for a Spanish
discovery of the Falklands decided that the islands were
the Falklands.

Had Pigafetta, the chronicler of Magellan's voyage and
one of the few survivors, been called to the 1522
Valladolid commission of enquiry into the voyage, he
could have made all clear, as his account does, that these
islands were nowhere near the Strait, but well up the
Patagonian coast, probably in the region of Bahia
Blanca. The names given to these islands and latched on
to the Falklands — Islas de los Patos and Islas de Sanson
— sometimes the two combined, arose from a confusion
of thought regarding the activities of the expedition as it

voyaged down the Patagonian coast.

Pigafetta makes clear in his account that not only did the expedition coast along the land all the way from the estuary of the Plate to the Strait but that the two islands, where they stopped by to load up with fat goslings (patos), as they described the penguins, were on the way to the next stop in 49½° (the first latitudinal reference he gives), which was Port St Julian where they stayed five months and met the giants (the Sansons), who were the Tehuelche Indians. At 51° (Santa Cruz) they spent another two months before continuing along the coast to the Strait. One apologist for a Spanish discovery of the Falklands even goes so far as to say that, while at Santa Cruz, Magellan sent out a ship to discover the islands, as if a ship hugging the land in a world unknown would venture forth in such a fashion.

Argentina, in its Statement to the UN Decolonisation Committee, submitted in 1964, says that discovery of the islands 'must be attributed to' Esteban Gomez, one of Magellan's captains, who deserted him in the Strait and returned home to Spain with news of its discovery. No proof of this attribution is forthcoming or why a captain, intent on taking his ship home, should venture so far east to make discovery.

In his map of the region, published in the 1600 edition of his Works, Hakluyt correctly identifies Magellan's islands as close to the Patagonian coast. He names them the Sanson Islands.

Davis' discovery of the Falklands was confirmed in 1594 when Sir Richard Hawkins sailed along their northern shores; but he did not land. 'The want of a pinnace disabled us for finding a port or rode, not being discretion with a ship of charge in an unknown coast to come near the shore before it was sounded.' A change of wind enabling him 'to pass the Streights' stopped further discovery. He gives, however, the first description of the land, 'a goodly champion country much of the disposition of England and as temperate'. He named it Hawkins Maiden-land, after Queen Elizabeth I.

Apologists for a Spanish discovery of the islands, armed with ammunition provided by a Commander Chambers, who wrote an article in the *Geographical Journal* in 1901, in which he purported to show that 'the evidence of Hawkins ever having visited the islands is entirely insufficient', proceeded to dispute Hawkins' discovery. Groussac, an Argentine historian, went even further, asserting that Hawkins came across Jane's account of the Davis discovery some fifteen months prior to the date of his own alleged visit and wrote his account from a confused mass of recollections of his experiences off the Patagonian coast. Hawkins, after leaving the Falklands, was captured by the Spanish off the Peruvian coast. He sent the account of his voyage home a year after his imprisonment but the book was not published until 1622, a year after his death.

The Groussac interpretation was accepted by Julius Goebel in his *Struggle for the Falklands* (1971). He, in turn, attributed the discovery of the islands to an unknown ship of the Camargo expedition of 1540. In his role of armchair navigator, he makes a plausible case, from the fragment of log available, that the ship wintered in the Falklands. In his book *Cape Horn* (1950) Felix Riesenberg, an American navigator, who rounded the Horn several times, identified the land where the unknown ship wintered as part of Tierra del Fuego which bears a distinct resemblance to the Falklands.

In 1925 the Governor of the Falklands took the opportunity of the visit to the islands of around the world yachtsman, Conor O'Brien, to have him make a professional assessment of Hawkins' voyage from Hawkins' own references, and reconstruct his track on the chart. After an examination of the courses steered by Hawkins, the winds and currents, O'Brien came to the conclusion that it was indeed the Falklands that Hawkins saw and skirted. Despite this Argentina continues to refer to Hawkins' discovery as hypothetical.

A name was given to the outlying Jason group by Sebald de Weert, the commander of one of the ships of

the Dutch de Mahu expedition, when, after being
beleaguered in the Strait, he was forced to return home
and sighted the group in January 1600 as he sailed by.
Continental map-makers, after his return, appended his
name for the Jasons, Sebaldes, to the whole archipelago.

In the early seventeeth century the Western Powers of
the time (Britain, France and Holland) were more
interested in carving out slices of the Spanish empire in
the Caribbean and North America than coming to the far
south. One venture at colonisation in the Strait was,
however, attempted by Sir John Narborough, acting on
instructions from Charles II, with a view to coming to an
arrangement with the Indians to exploit the hoped-for
minerals in the area. At that time the Spanish writ
extended only a short distance outside Buenos Aires,
beyond which the country was Indian-inhabited. The
idea of Britain colonising the Strait region had been put
forward after Drake's circumnavigation but had come to
nothing. Narborough's practical attempt also came to
nothing but his visit to the area was to have a Falkland
connection, in that the navigational and geographical
discoveries he made were to enable Captain Byron, who
eventually led the first expedition from Britain to the
Falklands, to save his life when his ship, part of the 1740
Anson expedition into the South Seas, was wrecked in the
Strait region.

In 1684 Dampier and Cowley, two buccaneering
scribes aboard the *Batchelor's Delight,* sailed by the Jason
group on their way to the South Seas. Dampier, in his
account, placed the islands in their correct latitude,
Cowley incorrectly in 41°40'. The editor of Cowley's
journal, unaware, as Cowley was, that Dampier had
correctly recorded their whereabouts, decided to drop the
40' and Cowley's conjecture that the islands might be the
Sebaldes and decided to treat the land seen as a new
discovery. He named it Pepys Island after the Secretary of
the Admiralty and, for good measure, appended an
Admiralty Bay and a Secretary's Point. The result was
that for nearly a century his mythical island appeared on

nautical charts and navigators looked for it in vain.

The first landing of which there is certain knowledge was made in 1690 from the English sloop, *Welfare,* commanded by John Strong who, on a privateering cruise against the French, then at war with England, was driven by westerly winds among the islands. Strong identified and sailed along the sound between East and West Falkland, naming it Falkland Sound, after the First Lord of the Admiralty.

In the period between the Treaty of Ryswick (1697) and the start of the Spanish War of Succession in 1704, and for some time after, many French ships came into the South Atlantic, operating at first under the aegis of a French company trading with Spanish Pacific ports, later, legally and illegally, under the Assiento, the contract to supply slaves to Buenos Aires which the French acquired in 1706. Many of these ships resorted to the islands to take on water and revive their scurvy-ridden crews, the islands being a rich source of the plant (scurvy grass) that made this possible. Several of these ships identified new parts of the archipelago. An important discovery by one of these ships was Beauchene Island, south of the Falklands, named after her captain. The French also gave the archipelago a new name, Iles Malouines, after St. Malo, the port from which most of the French ships came.

In 1708 an English privateer, Woode Rogers, later to become Governor of Jamaica, named the group Falkland's Land.

The first to appreciate the importance of the islands was George (later Lord) Anson who, writing in 1740, after his return from an expedition into the South Seas against the Spanish, suggested that the Admiralty should send a ship to survey them and Pepys Island, the ghost of which was not laid until some years later. 'It is scarcely to be conceived of what prodigious import a convenient station might prove, situated so far to the southward and so near Cape Horn.' The ships of the Woode Rogers expedition, he pointed out, took thirty-five days to reach

Juan Fernandez Island in the Pacific from the Falklands:

As the returning back is much facilitated by the western winds, I doubt not but a voyage might be made from Falkland's Isles to Juan Fernandez and back again in a little more than two months. This, even in time of peace, might be of great consequence to this nation and in time of war would make us masters of the sea.

Chapter 2

Initial Settlement

The first person to pursue Anson's suggestion that a closer inspection should be made of Falkland's Land, as the islands continued to be called until 1766, when they were renamed Falkland Islands, was Anson himself. After joining the Admiralty, he convinced them of the islands' strategic importance and in 1749, with the approval of the King, two frigates were got ready in the Thames to make an inspection.

The Spanish Ambassador in London heard of this and objected. Not to the main purpose of the expedition which was to make a full discovery of Pepys and Falkland Islands, but to the secondary intention to explore the South Seas. If the ships went to Juan Fernandez Island, as they would require to do for watering and wooding, they would come into too close proximity to the Spanish Pacific coast which 'could occasion suspicion and uneasiness between the two nations'.

The Government then took the unusual step of submitting the plan of the expedition to the Spanish Government whose chief objection was that to proceed with the expedition would give rise to 'future inconveniences'. At that time what became the Commerical Treaty of 1750 was being negotiated. England hoped to gain much by it. In the circumstances it would therefore have been unwise to despatch an expedition to a part of the world where Spain would prefer she did not go. It was accordingly cancelled.

England then gained a 'substantial improvement' in her existing commercial privileges in Spain and the English company which had held the Assiento, the contract to supply slaves to Buenos Aires, for the past twenty-five years, was handsomely compensated for its cancellation.

Argentina, in her Statement to the United Nations, gives as the reason for the withdrawal of the expedition a recognition by Britain of the 'rights of Spain over the islands and coast of South America in areas where British ships could neither sail or trade'. The only right Spain held at this time was that deriving from coastal discovery. Those accruing to her under the Papal Bull, which in the late fifteenth century had donated the world medially between Spain and Portugal, had by 1749 become defunct. At the time the Treaty of London was concluded in 1604 James I asserted that England would respect Spain's monopoly of trade and settlements in all territories effectively occupied by her but could recognise none in unoccupied territory. At this point in time the unoccupied Falkland Islands were a thousand miles away from the nearest point of the Spanish Vice-royalty.

The concept of 'closed seas', also deriving from Papal donation, was one Spain endeavoured to cling to long after the Spanish Ambassador in London, when he complained of Drake's voyage, was told by Queen Elizabeth that no right to the ocean can inure to any people since neither nature nor any reason of public use permits occupation of the ocean.

A tendency, which was to become a characteristic of the Spanish approach to the Falklands, of making assertive statement before producing known fact, made its first appearance at a meeting in 1749 between the British Ambassador and the Spanish Minister when the latter informed the British envoy that Pepys and Falkland Islands had been first discovered and inhabited by Spaniards and Spain had ample descriptions of their dimensions and properties.

If, in England, the idea of mounting an expedition to the islands had been temporarily set aside it was otherwise in France. A young French nobleman, Antoine Louis de Bougainville, who had read Anson's book, and, as aide de camp to Montcalm, witnessed France's humiliating defeat at Quebec, returned home determined to recoup his country for the loss of its North American colony by establishing a new one in these strategic islands. Obtaining the permission of the Duc de Choiseul, the French Foreign Minister, he embarked his fortune and that of several of his relatives in the enterprise. A frigate and a sloop were fitted out at St. Malo and on 1 September 1763 the expedition sailed, taking the first settlers, several refugee familes from Arcadia (Canada). The ships called at Montevideo to take on board cattle, horses, pigs and poultry. On 31 January 1764 they reached the islands.

The account of the Bougainville colonisation which Dom Pernety, the priest who accompanied the expedition, chronicled must surely rank as one of the most delightful accounts of a pioneering group arriving in a new land and especially in the Falklands where most of the information which has come down the years has been denigratory. There is no mention in the Pernety account of the perverse nature and weather which was to reach its apotheosis in the rich malevolent prose of the pamphlet Dr Samuel Johnson was commissioned to write to bolster the case for the faction in the Government who, in the 1770 Spanish-British imbroglio over the islands, were seeking to propagate their uselessness.

In some respects the French colonisation of the islands has the air of a picnic in an accidentally-discovered part of nature filled with the most agreeable surprises. We see Pernety toiling through the hummocky hay, bayonet at the end of his rifle, to deal with the wild animals, then discovering all are tame. We see him take his swig of brandy to revive himself when the hot summer's day becomes too much. We see him making his peat fire to prove to the others that the 'turf' he had discovered will provide the fuel they will need in a land of no trees, and M de Bougainville 'so anxious lest it should not prove the right kind of turf declaring in his opinion it was not', and then happy surprise. Happy surprise again when the animals put ashore near to death were found next day dispersed in the country fit and well. Everything is delightful discovery from local goodies, like wild celery and strawberries, to their own more gourmet ones that sea-lion tongue is preferable to ox or calf, penguin ragouts as good as hare, and bustard, as they called the upland goose, exquisite boiled, roasted or fricasseed.

As soon as the expedition moved on shore work was begun on the fort and the apartment house, the former being completed three weeks later when it was named Fort St Louis, and the first cannon mounted and fired. At the end of another three weeks the apartment house was completed and on 5 April the ceremony of taking possession took place. M de Bougainville presented the King's Commission to M de Nerville, his cousin, who was to remain as governor. Dom Pernety conducted the service and afterwards 'Vive le Roi' was shouted seven times and a salute of twenty-one cannon fired. Then they all went to the apartment house for a 'plentiful breakfast' after which there was an inspection of the seed beds, planted ten days before, which were found 'sprung up and in a healthy and flourishing state'.

Twenty-eight people were left behind when the ships returned to France. In October this number was increased to eighty when the frigate returned after the southern winter to find the settlement flourishing, everyone healthy, the kitchen garden flourishing, the cattle 'fat as hogs' living out-of-doors in all seasons. So little snow had fallen in the winter it had scarcely covered the shoe buckles.

On this visit Bougainville sailed to the mainland to make contact with 'their nearest neighbours', the Indians of Patagonia, whom he found well-disposed and friendly. He returned with tree seedlings for the colony, 'having opened up a seaway necessary for the support of the colony'.

A return visit from France towards the end of the year increased the number of colonists to 150. The ship took back a cargo of oil and sealskins.

The deferred British expedition finally got under way in June 1764, under the command of Captain John Byron. It sailed unaware of the establishment of the

French settlement, news of which did not become public until the following August. The Admiralty, determined this time that there would be no interference from the Cabinet, who had been responsible for the previous referral to the Spanish Government, refrained from informing the Government of their intentions. Only the King was made privy to these. Also, to hoodwink the Brazilian authorities when they put into Rio for refreshments and repair, the destination up to that point had been described as the East Indies, it being customary for ships bound east to call in at Brazil. No news of the expedition leaked out in Britain until July 1765, when Lord Egmont, First Lord of the Admiralty, informed Lord Grafton of 'the re-discovery of the Falklands'.

Byron reached the islands on 12 January 1765. After a vain search for Pepys Island, when he came to the conclusion there was no such island in the latitude and longitude laid down, he came to anchor in the north-west of the archipelago at what is now Saunders Island, in what he described as one of the finest harbours in the world. 'The whole navy of England', he wrote, 'might ride here in perfect security from all winds'. He named the harbour Port Egmont, after the First Lord. He was impressed by what he saw when he landed. The soil was extremely good, 'covered all over with wood sorrel and wild celery, the best antiscorbutiks, in the world'. There was nothing lacking but wood.

On 23 January he took formal possession. 'The Union Jack was erected on a high staff', he reported, 'and being spread I named the whole His Majesty's Isles which I claimed for the Crown of Great Britain, his heirs and successors'.

Four days later he sailed from Port Egmont to continue his own voyage of exploration, travelling eastwards along the north coast, naming the geographical features as he passed them. The Sound, at the head of which, unknown to him, was the French settlement, he named Berkeley. He noted that it had an opening which had the appearance of a harbour.

A few days later in the Strait of Magellan an opportunity occurred for him to meet Bougainville but Byron did not take it. Sighting a strange sail which 'caused them some alarm as it appeared to be following them', he came to anchor to determine, if he could, what it was. His storeship, trying to anchor nearby, ran aground whereupon the strange sail hoisted French colours and launched two boats to assist her. Byron, however, refused the assistance, the storeship being released by his own boats. The strange sail was carrying Bougainville on his goodwill visit to the Patagonians. He, on his side, did not discover what the other strange sail was as Byron sailed off without hoisting colours.

The next British expedition sailed from England in September 1765, under the command of Captain John McBride, and comprised the frigate *Jason,* the sloop *Carcass* and the storeship *Experiment.* Its purpose, besides establishing a permanent foothold on the islands, was to seek out 'any lawless person' — the British Government was now aware the French were on the islands — 'who was to be requested to leave or take the oath of allegiance to HM Government'. Inhabitants of 'any foreign settlement' were to be given six months to leave. One of the ships was to remain permanently at Port Egmont, the other to coast around the islands, exploring and making surveys of the interior as well as of the coast.

McBride was an unfortunate choice as leader of such an expedition. His interests were nautical. Landward he had none. He contradicted Byron. The prospect was dreary — a range of barren mountains heightened by almost constant gales of wind. The soil was all bog, the land destitute of wood. He described the penguins and sea lions as vermin. Gardens had been planted, he reported, but he set no store by them. They had, in fact, it was discovered later, been planted in the worst possible position, facing south to Antarctica.

Only the port facilities impressed him. A squadron arriving in the right season (November) would find some refreshment from 'what nature had thrown up on them', such as geese, snipe, wild celery and fish. It was from McBride's gloomy reports that Dr. Johnson compiled his even gloomier appraisal of the islands.

In November the ship engaged on survey discovered the French settlement. McBride proceeded to Berkeley Sound but owing to contrary winds could not get up to the settlement. He sent a note to the French commandant informing him that the islands were first discovered by Britain, that they belonged to His Majesty and enquiring on what authority they had erected a settlement. De Nerville, who spoke no English, requested, in his turn, that McBride explain in the French language what he was doing there. McBride explained and was told he would not be allowed to enter. He replied that his orders were to examine the islands and he would do this. He requested that one of his officers be allowed to examine the French settlement. He was told this would not be allowed. Then the wind shifted. McBride took his ship up. There was more altercation but eventually the French gave way.

McBride went ashore. The authority for the settlement, a commission from Louis XV, dated 1 August 1764, which had been granted to Bougainville on his return to France, was produced. McBride then inspected the settlement, describing it as consisting of seventeen houses; the Governor's was the only one of stone, the rest being of peat thatched with sedge (tussac, the indigenous Falkland grass). There were 130 men, women and children in the settlement which possessed three schooners. McBride gave them orders to leave. The commandant replied that he would not do so unless compelled by force. There the matter rested.

Unofficially the visit was a great success. The British told the French of their colony, its fine harbour, its armoury, the explorations they had made. McBride was invited to visit de Nerville in his house and de Nerville to dine on board the *Jason*. However, a favourable wind springing up cut short the exchange of hospitality.

While all this was taking place the French colony had in fact passed into Spanish hands. The Spanish

Government, on learning through its agents in Montevideo of the establishment of the colony, instructed its ambassador in Paris to inform the French Government that the Family Compact, recently concluded between the two countries, did not authorise such a one-sided action. Choiseul replied that the ships had gone to discover an island which would facilitate passage around the Horn and the commander was aware he had no right to enter Spanish colonies or traffic with them. The visit to Montevideo had been occasioned by necessity of repairs (which, by a stretch of meaning, could be made to include the taking aboard of animals). Choiseul was then informed that a French settlement 'at this place' was prejudicial as it would be a signal to Britain to undertake a similar expedition. France was formally requested to abandon it.

Weakened after the Seven Years' War, dependent on its alliance with Spain, France capitulated. Bougainville, on return from his second visit to the islands, was despatched to Madrid to negotiate what, to him, was a contract of surrender, the sale of his settlement for £25,000. The date was 4 October 1766.

The disposition of Spain to make assertive statement before adducing fact was revealed again in the wording of the document Bougainville was required to sign. It referred to his establishments in the Iles Malouines as being illegitimate as the islands *belonged to His Catholic Majesty.* Which they could not and did not.

The formal act of cession took place at Port Louis on 1 April 1767.

Bougainville never recognised that the Spanish had any claim to the islands. Throughout his life he referred to it as 'imaginary'.

Chapter 3

The Spanish Intrusion

The Spanish occupation of East Falkland, which lasted until 1811, can claim one distinctive achievement — it so successfully generated the idea that the islands were a worthless place that the impression was not only to persist in the years immediately following the Spaniards' departure but to travel down the years, affect British colonisation and colour thinking about the islands ever since.

The Spanish authorities on the mainland saw the islands solely in a Papal Bull context, as a piece of territory in an area they regarded as theirs, from which all other Powers, particularly Britain, had to be excluded. The islands to them were simply a place to hold. The only population necessary for this being a garrison, that became the only population, apart from the convicts in the penal settlement when that was built. The garrison never numbered more than 120. In overall charge of the guard-post, or colony as they euphemistically named it — there never were any women in it — was a Governor who was also commander of the island schooner. The islands were so ill-regarded that no Governor, despite double pay, could be persuaded to serve longer than his required time.

The first arrivals in 1767 behaved like passengers from a luxury liner marooned on an alien shore. Uprooted from their town-based mainland colonial life and dumped on a featureless land at the start of winter, they felt they had come to the end of the earth. 'I tarry in this unhappy desert,' wrote the chaplain accompanying them, 'suffering all for the love of God.' His words could have served as the motto of the Spanish throughout their entire stay. They gave East Falkland the uncheerful name of Soledad (solitude). The French Port Louis became Port Soledad.

Don Ruiz Puente, the first Governor at Soledad, and Captain Anthony Hunt, now in charge of the British establishment on West Falkland, describe the islands in their first reports in almost identical terms. Neither could get vegetables to grow but both were impressed with what Hunt called the good herbage for sheep and goats, and Puente the fine pasture for cattle. To ensure themselves a constant supply of sustenance from the latter, the Spanish augmented the stock of sixty cows and six horses the French had left with importations from the coast. By 1782 the cattle had multiplied to 534, the horses to 50. They were to go on multiplying, particularly after the Spanish left, to become the source of the political complications which were to beset the islands in the nineteenth century and subsequently.

Coastal surveys being an activity carried out from both settlements, it was inevitable that at some stage the respective parties would meet and collide politically. In September 1769 Captain Hunt was making a cruise around the islands when he met a Spanish schooner. Hunt enquired of the captain what he was doing there and was told he had been sent out by the Governor of the Spanish settlement. Hunt gave him formal notice to leave the islands.

The schooner sailed off but, two days later, joined Hunt in an East Falkland harbour. On board was a Spanish officer with two letters for Hunt from the Governor. In one Ruiz Puente expressed astonishment that the schooner's voyage had been interrupted and enquired 'if this was due to some act on the part of the master for he could hardly think an officer of Hunt's rank, commanding a ship of war of so civilised a nation, would so flagrantly offend against the respect due to the King, my Master's flag, especially within his dominions'. The second letter gave Hunt formal notice to leave the islands.

Hunt replied that the islands belonged to His Britannic Majesty, his Master, by right of discovery as well as settlement. He gave Puente formal notice to leave within six months.

While this was happening two Spanish frigates were, in fact, on their way from Buenos Aires to Port Egmont, with two English deserters acting as guides, to expel the English. Until he got hold of the English seamen Don Francisco de Paula Bucareli, the Buenos Aires Governor, had been unable to find the English settlement which the Madrid Government had told him was 'in these waters'. He had been searching in the region of Tierra del Fuego, being directed there after the captain of Bougainville's frigate had assured Madrid that, if the English were on the islands, they could not be found. The Spanish ships called first at Port Soledad where Fernando Rubalcava, the commander, learned of the encounter with Hunt.

On 20 February he arrived at Port Egmont to find not one frigate, as he expected, but three — *Tamar, Favourite* and *Swift* — and the storeship *Florida*. Faced with a superior force, Rubalcava sent a letter ashore, expressing surprise at finding an English settlement 'which was in violation of treaties which allowed no intrusion into the King of Spain's dominions' but he would abstain from any proceeding until he had acquainted His Catholic Majesty with the disagreeable affair and received his royal orders concerning it. Except for the reference to treaties, this was in strict accord with the instructions issued to Bucareli by the Madrid Government in February 1768. Expulsion of the 'unpermitted' English establishment was only to be carried out when the Spanish force could do so effectively.

The Spanish frigates remained in port for a further eight days, taking soundings and making plans of the port and shore establishments. Hunt invited the commander and his officers ashore but they declined.

When the news reached Bucareli he did not bother to wait for the royal instructions. He ordered five frigates, recently arrived from Spain, to sail to the islands and expel the English.

The first ship, the *Industria,* with the commodore, Captain Juan Madariaga, aboard, reached Port Egmont on 4 June to find only one English ship, the *Favourite,* under command of Captain George Farmer, in port. The *Tamar* and *Florida* had sailed for England in March. The *Swift* had been wrecked on the Patagonian coast, Captain Maltby and his crew augmenting the much reduced garrison.

Madariaga asked for water, saying he had been twenty-three days from Buenos Aires and was bound for Port Soledad. After watering, however, he made no move to go. Three days later the rest of the squadron arrived. Madariaga then hoisted the Spanish broad pennant and sent two notes ashore to the respective captains requesting them to quit or he would be obliged to resort to hostilities. He followed this up next day with a note to the two captains jointly. No colonies, he told them, could be made in the region without the consent of the Spanish king. He demanded they withdraw. Farmer made what dispositions he could to defend the settlement and then, boldly, sent a message to Madariaga requesting him to depart since he had received the refreshment he had come for. Madariaga replied requesting Farmer to send an officer to view the troops he had for landing. The officer reported back that Madariaga had 1600 seamen and a train of artillery sufficient to reduce a regular fortification. By now the Spanish frigates had moved inshore and moored opposite the blockhouse.

On 10 June a party of Spanish troops and artillery landed half a mile from the settlement. At the same time the remainder of the troops put off from one of the frigates covered by fire. The English fired some shot then 'not seeing the least probability of being able, against such a superior force, to defend the settlement, hoisted a flag of truce and desired articles of capitulation which were in part granted.'

Under these the English surrendered the blockhouse and the rest of the settlement. They were permitted to fly their flag until embarkation and to take away everything moveable but not allowed to sail for twenty days after the departure of the Spanish frigates, one of which, the *Industria,* sailed to Spain with news of the expulsion of the English. To ensure delay, the rudder of the *Favourite* was removed. It sailed eventually for England on 14 July, arriving on 22 September. The *Industria* had reached Cadiz on 12 August.

Bucareli had achieved what Spain desired — but in the wrong manner. The situation had to be righted so that what the Governor had done too precipitately could be achieved by less obvious means.

The first step was to anticipate the bellicose intentions which the English would express when they got the full details on the *Favourite's* return. This was done by first preventing news of the incident from leaking out at the Spanish end and then instructing their Ambassador in London, Prince Masserano, to inform the British Government that there was a possiblity that the Buenos Aires Governor, Bucareli, might be sending a large squadron of frigates to Port Egmont to force the British out. It was the hope of the Spanish Government that, should this prove to be so, such acts executed by Bucareli without royal authority would not lead the British Government to take measures dangerous to the good understanding between the two Crowns. The British chargé d'affaires in Madrid, Harris, was fobbed off with a sight of a supposed reply from the Spanish Government to a recently-received letter from Bucareli about the February events and intimating that another expedition was planned, which ordered him to desist.

On receipt of the British Note demanding disavowal of Bucareli and restitution of the settlement at Port Egmont to *status quo ante,* the Spanish Government announced it would be sending a set of proposals to their Ambassador in London where the matter should be settled — not in Madrid where, diplomatically, it ought to have been. The British Government made no protest over this — it had also made no protest over the Rubalcava incident. It was, Choiseul said, the weakest British Government in history. The Prime Minister, Lord North, had a reputation for vacillation.

In the convention which Spain proposed should be
drawn up the whole responsibility for what Bucareli had
done was placed on poor Captain Hunt whom she
described as 'the menace'. Had he not behaved as he did
Bucareli would not have acted as he did. Spain was
willing to disavow 'any particular orders to Bucareli' but
at the same time it was to be acknowledged that he had
acted in accordance with general instructions and on his
oath as Governor. Had Britain acknowledged this it
would have amounted to inferential acceptance of
Spanish colonial laws and thereby of Spanish rights to the
islands. Spain undertook to restore Port Egmont but
without prejudice to her rights to the islands. Finally she
raised the subject of evacuation, proposing that the two
powers should evacuate at a time to be fixed — not
mutually — but by the British. The latter's request in
their Note that Spain should convey the settlers back was
flatly rejected as the question of sovereignty would have
been compromised. Spain had deftly thrown the onus of
the situation on to the British to be resolved in their
country.

Masserano was told to delay negotiations as far as
possible and to raise hopes for an accommodation, in
order to avoid a declaration of war by Britain before
Spain had advanced her own war preparations which had
been begun immediately following the return of
Madariaga.

Masserano delayed negotiations so successfully that
eventually the Secretary of State, Lord Weymouth,
refused to carry on negotiating. Weymouth, probably the
strongest man in the North administration, wanted
nothing but a direct response to the British demands.

At this stage, Frances, who had until recently been
French chargé d'affaires in London, entered the scene,
supposedly sent by the new French Ambassador Comte
de Guines to sound North on the situation following
Weymouth's intransigence.

Frances had extraordinary luck. It was then late
November 1770, the two sides had been re-arming

steadily, France (Spain's ally) less so, as Choiseul was having difficulty with his Government who could perhaps see no virtue in going to war over a territory which Spain had grabbed from them. North did not want war — some said because he did not want to lose power which he would have done had the situation deteriorated. He was therefore receptive to whatever Frances had to say, which was exclusively on evacuation.

It is clear that what North meant by evacuation was evacuation of occupation — a discontinuance temporarily of a settlement which McBride's reports had revealed as not worth maintaining — not evacuation at the same time of his country's right to the islands which Frances, by steering the talks in the direction of the evacuation of West Falkland, endeavoured to contrive. It was the loose fashion in which North expressed himself, his vehement reiterances that 'England did not want the island, it was of no use to us', albeit always accompanied by the words 'unofficial' and 'without guarantee', in these exchanges with a Frenchman who was not an official representative of Spain, that was to lead to the assertion, advanced on the Spanish side, that a secret verbal promise had been made by England whereby she would evacuate the islands in all respects after a brief return stay.

Weymouth, who had been trying unsuccessfully to induce North to stop talking with Frances and recall Harris from Madrid, resigned in mid-December. A more important departure at the end of the month was that of Choiseul who was dismissed by Louis XV at the behest of his mistress, Madame du Barry. Louis then wrote to Charles III advising against war. The result was a new suggested Declaration from the Spanish Government to Masserano — it had been agreed between Frances and North that the document of settlement should take the form of a Declaration from Spain to which Britain would reply in a Counter Declaration.

This Declaration provided for what Britain had originally asked, restitution and disavowal, the latter, however, not of Bucareli by name but 'of the violent enterprise'. There was also a vital alteration in the phrasing obtained by Britain in the discussions with Masserano prior to signing. What, in the original Spanish version, was 'shall not prejudice anterior rights of His Catholic Majesty to the islands' became in the final version 'cannot nor ought in any wise to affect the question of the prior right of sovereignty of the islands'.

Nevertheless, when the documents finally appeared towards the end of January 1771, the Earl of Chatham was bothered by this phrasing and sought the advice of the ex-Lord Chief Justice, Lord Camden, on whether 'a restitution made by the King of Spain to the King of England under a reservation of a disputed right of sovereignty could be accepted and carried into execution without derogation of the law touching the interest and essential dignity of the Crown'.

In his reply, Lord Camden said such reservation in no way touched the right of the King of Great Britain. His right of sovereignty was absolute from the moment restitution was made, his title not abridged or limited, as reservation neither denied the title on one side nor asserted it on the other. The situation was as before the hostility, the King of Spain declaring only that he ought not to be precluded from his former claim by this act of possessory restitution.

There was more disputation when the actual process of repossession came to be discussed. The Spanish suggestion that the British ships should go to Port Soledad to receive possession was rejected by Britain who saw in it an attempt on the Spanish side to get inferential recognition of their right to the islands. If the British ships had to go to Soledad they would have to adhere to the instructions given to Byron and inform the Spanish squadron they must leave as the islands belonged to the British king. Eventually the matter was resolved by Spain arranging for an officer from Soledad to go to Port Egmont to be there when the British ships arrived to take repossession.

The three British ships, the frigate *Juno,* under command of Captain Stott, the sloop *Hound* and the storeship *Florida,* arrived at Port Egmont on 13 September. Restitution was formally made to Captain Stott on the 15th. The transaction, he reported, was made with the greatest appearance of good faith, without the least claim being made by the Spanish officer on behalf of his Court.

The settlement continued at Port Egmont for only a further three years. When it withdrew the Spanish asserted this was because of the supposed secret promise made in 1770, but it is clear from the remarks of North and his ministers to Frances and Masserano, subsequent to the signing of the Declarations, that evacuation of occupancy was to have been reciprocal and to take place within two years. The 1774 evacuation had nothing to do with evacuation in the terms in which it had been discussed with, principally, Frances. It had to do, as Secretary of State Lord Rochford said at the time, with a retraction of naval forces in overseas stations.

Before the British departed on 20 May 1774, a lead plaque was fixed to the blockhouse door expressing British ownership:

Be it known to all nations that Falkland's Islands, with this fort, the storehouse, wharfs, harbours, bays and creeks thereunto belonging, are the sole property of His Most Sacred Majesty, George the Third, King of Great Britain, France and Ireland, Defender of the Faith. In witness whereof this plate is set up, and His Britannic Majesty's colours left flying as a mark of possession by S. W. Clayton, Commanding officer at Falkland's Islands, AD 1774.

They left behind thirty-eight gardens in a sheltered valley a mile from the settlement where, disproving the McBrides and Hunts, they had grown every kind of vegetable, except peas 'which the mice ate'.

Five years later, the Spanish in Port Soledad, on orders from Madrid, demolished the settlement at Port Egmont. The plaque was taken to Buenos Aires where it remained in Government archives until the British invasion in 1806.

After 1811 until November 1820 the only people on the islands were the itinerant sealers.

Chapter 4

The Argentine Connection

On 1 November 1820 Captain James Weddell, the Antarctic explorer and sealer, at anchor in the *Jane* in Berkeley Sound, observed a battered frigate, the *Heroina*, come to anchor nearby. Weddell was invited aboard, the commander, Daniel Jewittt, receiving him with extreme politeness. Understanding, Weddell reports, that he could conduct his ship up the sound to the main anchorage, Jewitt begged his favour to move it. Seeing the nature of the *Heroina* — it was a Buenos Aires privateer, Jewitt, one of the many soldiers of fortune then in the employ of the patriot government — and the lack of men aboard (nearly half the ship's complement had died or were sick of scurvy) which could mean were he unaccommodating Jewitt might seize his own crew, Weddell complied.

Arriving at Port Soledad too late in the day to return to his own anchorage, Weddell spent the night aboard, sharing a cabin with Jewitt who slept, he noted, in his trousers a dirk belted round him and a pair of pistols over his head. He told Weddell he had been eight months at sea, had crossed the equator to the Cape Verde Islands and taken a prize.

Two days later Jewitt sent a letter to all sealing masters in port informing them that he had been commissioned by the Supreme Government of the United Provinces of South America to 'take possession of these islands in the name of the country to which they naturally appertain'.

Weddell was in no doubt that Jewitt's principal business in putting in to the islands was to refresh his crew and that taking possession was subsidiary. This view would seem to have been borne out by the circumstances. The un-United Provinces were in a state of unrest. There was no Supreme Government. There were in the year

1820 at least twenty-four governments. Described by Argentine historians as 'the terrible year', it was the most anarchical in Argentina's early history. It is highly unlikely that one of these governments, during its brief reign, would have had time to think of the islands let alone despatch Jewitt to take possession. It seems more probable that Jewitt, having heard at sea or indeed before he set out — Weddell had only Jewitt's word for it that he had been eight months at sea — of the news brought to Montevideo in April by French naturalists, the de Freycinets, had taken it upon himself to take possession of the islands on behalf of the United Provinces, which act was afterwards confirmed by the Buenos Aires Government. This is the view taken by F. A. Kirkpatrick in his *History of the Argentine Republic.* The de Freycinets had been marooned on East Falkland for two months after their ship, the *Uranie,* struck the Volunteer Rocks at the entrance to Berkeley Sound on the last lap of their three-year botanical cruise around the world. The news they brought to Montevideo was that the island was teeming with wild cattle and horses — important news because the cattle business, as the slaughtering of the wild cattle for their hides and tallow was called, was then a highly profitable activity on the mainland.

Jewitt took formal possession on 6 November, reading a declaration under the Provinces' colours planted on the ruined fort. A twenty-one gun salute was fired. Jewitt's officers, some of whom, like most of his crew, had been taken out of prison, were in full uniform, described by Weddell as 'being exactly like that of our navy'. Jewitt struck such terror into some of the sealing masters lest they be robbed or captured that one of them proposed taking arms against him.

There were sixteen of these sealing vessels in Berkeley Sound when Jewitt arrived, forty more around the islands. In 1820 sealing activity in the South Atlantic was approaching its height. The islands, so conveniently situated, with their always-available supply of food, became a staging point for vessels bound to and from

Antarctica, at first to stop by, then to winter in and then to do sealing at. They had at that time very extensive rookeries of fur and elephant seals.

The rush south of the sealers had begun after Captain Cook's discovery in 1775 of the 'fabulous, fur-coated beaches' of South Georgia. The sealers were a constant plague to the Spanish at Port Soledad, paying no heed to their warnings that the islands and seas around belonged to Spain. Port Egmont, after its evacuation, became a kind of sealers' HQ. When the islands became wholly vacant, the sealers more or less took them over, destroying all kind of wild life besides seals. Penguining — the boiling down of penguins for their oil — was one of their subsidiary activities. Sealing, on a diminishing scale, continued until late in the nineteenth century when it was replaced as an extermination industry by whaling.

The North American sealers, who were in the majority, the others being British and French, came to regard their right to be on the islands as natural as their right to be in their own country. At one stage, when trouble erupted, as it did as soon as the islands were populated again, the US envoy in Buenos Aires informed his British opposite number that the USA, as a former colony of Britain, had inherited from her the right to seal around the Falklands.

In a not dissimilar fashion, Argentina was to maintain that she, as heir to Spain, had inherited the Falklands. Unlike British colonies, vice royalties were not regarded as possessions of the mother country but as direct dependencies of the Spanish Crown. When the Crown was in full authority this presented no difficulties but, after 1808, when Napoleon invaded Spain, deposing Charles IV and putting his brother Joseph on the throne, complications began. Joseph was naturally unacceptable in the Plate. So, too, in Buenos Aires was the Central Junta, the administrative end of the Council of Regency, which came into being in unoccupied south-west Spain, to govern on behalf of Charles's exiled son, Ferdinand, in whose favour he had renounced his throne. When news of Napoleon's successes against the Central Junta reached

Buenos Aires, the Viceroy the junta had appointed was ejected. On 25 May, 1810, the Vice-royalty was voted out and a local provisional junta formed which pledged itself to 'preserve this part of America for our august sovereign, Ferdinand VII'. Then, presuming inheritance of the entire former Vice-royalty, which included the Falklands, the islands having been incorporated into it on the formation of the Vice-royalty in 1776, the Junta despatched an armed force to the cities in the interior to ensure their adherence to the new state of things and was successful with all except Asuncion, soon to become capital of a separate country, Paraguay, and Montevideo, a very Spanish city, which had established its own direct link with the Council of Regency and had no wish to sever it. In 1811, when its ultra-royalist military Governor, Xavier Elio, returned from Spain in his new role of Viceroy of the Plate, he proceeded to prepare for an offensive against Buenos Aires but was stopped when his own hinterland erupted in a rebellion which was to lead to the eventual independence of Banda Oriental, now Uruguay.

The Buenos Aires Junta did not send an armed force to the Falklands to ensure their adhesion to the new state of affairs for the good reason presumably that there was still a Spanish garrison in occupation there. They took the simpler course of assuming inheritance of the islands.

In her Statement to the United Nations, Argentina explains the situation in a difficult-to-comprehend manner. In one part, she says 'Spain exercised dominion over the Malvinas Islands until the Revolution of 1810, which was the beginning of Argentine independence'. Elsewhere she says, 'Spain exercised effective possession of the islands until 1811'. What she would appear to be indicating is that dominion and possession are two quite different things. Spain held both dominion and possession up to 25 May, 1810. After that date she only had possession as, on that day, Argentina inherited dominion.

This interpretation does not appear to have been

shared by Spain. General Vigodet, the military Governor of Montevideo who, in January 1811, withdrew the Spanish garrison from the Falklands for reasons of economy, in 1818 was considering the islands as a place of sustenance for a contemplated expedition to subdue Buenos Aires.

Nor by Uruguay, a country which, as Spain's successor in the Banda Oriental, had a more comprehensible genealogical link to Spain's 'right' to the Falklands. In a dispute with Argentina in 1969 over islands in the River Plate, her delegate reminded his Argentina opposite number that if he got on to historical precedents, Uruguay would establish her claim to the Falklands and, when she did, would acknowledge British sovereignty.

In April 1820 as news of the Falkland riches reached Montevideo, Don Pacheco, whose cattle business had run into financial difficulties, approached Louis Vernet, a successful man of affairs in Buenos Aires, for help. In return, he promised him half of a large sum of money owed him by the Government.

Louis Vernet was no ordinary man of business. Not only able and scrupulous in all his dealings he was also cultured and far-seeing. The British consul in Buenos Aires described him to London as 'highly intelligent'. Born in France of Protestant parents who, after the Edict of Nantes, had taken up residence in Hamburg, where Vernet grew up, he was sent by his father at the age of fourteen to the United States to train in a business associated with his own. In the eight years he spent there he acquired a high reputation both for ability and quality of character. He came to Buenos Aires in 1817 after a spell in Lisbon.

The Government, when Pacheco requested repayment of his loan, was unable to oblige. Instead it offered him the usufruct of the cattle on East Falkland. Vernet, disinclined at first to accept, eventually agreed provided he took commercial control.

The first expedition, which sailed for the islands in 1823, was a failure. The fact that an Englishman was in charge would seem to have no political significance. Vernet said later that when he embarked on the enterprise he was unaware of any British claim to the islands. It seems unlikely he could have known, as Britain had done nothing to express her right to the islands for nearly fifty years. In 1823 there was no British representative in Buenos Aires.

Accompanying the expedition was Don Pablo Areguati, a retired captain of militia with whom Vernet had made a contract to go as Commandant of Soledad, to maintain 'the respect of labourers and foreign ships as well as to take possession of the islands'. It would seem Vernet set little store by the Jewitt effort or had not heard of it.

Vernet himself led the second expedition which sailed in 1826. It, too, almost ended in disaster. Several of the ships he bought and chartered were lost at sea with their valuable cargoes of horses for hunting down the wild cattle. He lost more horses when they were landed owing to change of climate and during training. Accustomed to the hard solid plains of Buenos Aires, they soon became disabled on the soft terrain of the Falklands. His partners refused to continue and sold him their shares. Vernet persevered, evolving a scientific method for the training and use of hunting horses so that by 1828 he had solved his 'horse problem' and was supplying an increasing number of ships with fresh and salted beef.

By now aware of what the islands could become, with their natural resources and superb situation on what he called the highway round Cape Horn, he applied to the Buenos Aires Government for permission to make a colony and was given a grant of all East Falkland, together with sole right to the seal fisheries. Also aware by now of the British claim to the islands, he submitted the official Grant of East Falkland, given by the Buenos Aires Government, to Woodbine Parrish, the British representative in Buenos Aires, who read it and stamped it with the Consular Seal. Parrish asked Vernet to prepare a detailed report on the islands which, with translations of the Grant, he sent to London. Vernet, on his side, told Parrish he would be happy if His Majesty's Government would take his settlement under its protection. This, too, was passed to London.

Armed with a grant from one country, officially endorsed by another, Vernet proceeded to form his colony. In the three years it was to endure, an ever-increasing number of ships were supplied with, besides beef, vegetables of all kinds and dairy produce. Dried beef and salted fish were exported to Brazil and wool to London which, though taken from sheep imported from Buenos Aires, fetched double the price of wool from there. Vernet made contracts in the United States and Europe to bring out families and acquire vessels to become the property of the colony without disbursement, as he put it, by paying for them out of the produce of the colony. By 1831 the wild cattle numbered 20,000, the settlers nearly ninety. He had eighty well-trained horses and he reckoned in two or three years he would have tamed all the wild cattle.

One of Captain Fitzroy's officers on the *Beagle,* who dined with Vernet around this time, described him as a man possessed of much information, who spoke several languages. In his house at Port Soledad he found a good library of Spanish, German and English works. In the room there was a grand pianoforte and in the evening they had music and dancing. Mrs Vernet gave some excellent singing which sounded not a little strange at the Falkland Islands where the visitors had expected to find only sealers.

The only obstacle to the continuing onward progress of the colony was the North American sealers who, with the Antarctic rookeries practically worked out, were coming around the island in increasing numbers. Vernet applied to the Buenos Aires Government for a man-of-war. It was again a time of upheaval on the mainland. The Government could not provide. Instead, it appointed him Governor. Vernet would have preferred a man-of-war. He told Woodbine Parrish he accepted the appointment only from fear that some creole officer would be appointed whose governorship would become detrimental to his private concerns. He accepted no pay. The Decree appointing him was made on 10 June, 1829, a date which, under the Peron administration, was to become transformed into a National Day of Affirmation (of Argentina's Right to the Falklands) and, as such, is now a day of annual celebration.

In November 1829 Parrish lodged a Protest with the Buenos Aires Government against its appointment of a governor in the Falklands pointing out that the British rights of ownership, founded upon original discovery and subsequent occupation, had acquired an additional sanction from the restoration by His Catholic Majesty in 1771. The withdrawal of HM's forces from the islands could not be considered as invalidating HM's just rights, being taken in pursuance of a system of retrenchment adopted at that time, but the marks and signals of possession and property had been left on the islands when the Governor took his departure. The flag had been left flying and all formalities observed which indicated the right of ownership as well as an intention to resume occupation of the territory at a more convenient time.

The presentation of this made no difference to Parrish's own relationship with Vernet. He continued to write and encourage him and Vernet continued to report on his progress.

After his appointment, Vernet issued warnings to the masters of sealing vessels cruising around the islands intimating that if caught unlawfully sealing after a first warning, the ship would be confiscated and the master taken to Buenos Aires for trial. In mid-1831 he seized the *Harriet,* a North American sealer, which had been warned twice, and took the ship to Buenos Aires.

The only US authority there at the time was a vitriolic consul who took the view that his country's sealers could seal where they pleased and should not be interfered with. Branding Vernet a pirate, he demanded that he be brought to trial and the US Government paid damages for the seizure of the *Harriet*. Then, at his instigation, and with the captain's collusion, the US corvette *Lexington* sailed to the islands and physically destroyed the settlement. Matthew Brisbane, whom Vernet had left in charge, was taken to Montevideo in irons, abused on the voyage and treated as a pirate. Brisbane, one of the unsung heroes of early Antarctic exploration, had come south with Weddell, helped him chart the South Shetlands, and had himself sailed farther south than Captain Cook. He joined Vernet in 1830 after being shipwrecked on Tierra del Fuego and making his way to the Falklands in an improvised boat.

The Buenos Aires Government, on behalf of Vernet, presented a claim to the US Government for 'satisfaction for the illegal character of the *Lexington* raid, reparation and indemnity.' The US Government countered with a claim for disavowal of Vernet, restoration of property and indemnity 'as the United States had been in actual use of the islands as a fishery for fifty years'. Vernet never got satisfaction. Nor his heirs when, in 1884, President Roca approached President Cleveland. The claim was dismissed as groundless.

Replacing Vernet, who had refused to return to the islands in such a capacity, Captain Juan Mestivier was appointed Governor towards the end of 1832. His reign was brief. Soon after arrival he was murdered by mutinous soldiers.

Captain Pinedo of the *Sarandi,* the ship which brought Mestivier to the islands, had just succeeded in capturing them when the British sloop *Clio* arrived. The British Government, alarmed at what had happened and, it was said, fearful of a North American sealer take-over, had decided to act. The Admiralty was ordered to instruct the Admiral on the South American station at Rio to take measures for 'periodically exercising the right of sovereignty on behalf of His Majesty over the Falkland Islands'.

The *Clio's* commanding officer, Captain Onslow, with two officers went on board the *Sarandi* and informed

Captain Pinedo that they had come to take possession of
the islands as belonging to His Majesty. They requested
him to haul down his flag and embark his force within
twenty-four hours. This was followed by an official letter
stating that the national flag of Great Britain would be
hoisted on shore next day 3 January 1833 when Pinedo
was requested to haul down the Argentine flag and
withdraw his force, taking all stores belonging to his
Government.

Pinedo refusing to lower his flag, it was struck and
delivered to the *Sarandi*. A flagstaff was put up at the
house of Vernet's storekeeper, William Dickson, who in
the absence of Brisbane was the senior British resident on
the islands, and the Union Jack hoisted.

Due to bad weather the *Sarandi* was unable to sail until
the 5th. It took away all the soldiers and convicts it had
brought down — the junta in Buenos Aires was intending
to resume settlement in the Spanish fashion — and those
of Vernet's remaining settlers[1] who also wished to leave.

This was the event which Argentina has described as
the forcible removal of that country's establishment on
the islands. The Buenos Aires Government, had been on
the islands a bare three months. It had never had any
direct association with the Vernet colony. It had provided
him with no garrision or authority other than, after 1829,
with a governorship he did not want.

---

[1] Argentina likes to stress that Argentine settlers were ousted and
replaced. This is incorrect. Those settlers who wished to leave were
allowed to go. The rest continued at the now renamed Port Louis. It is
significant that only a proportion of people at Vernet's settlement were
in fact from Argentina. A large number came from Banda Oriental.

Chapter 5

The British Repossession

The coming of the British ships — the *Tyne* arrived after the *Clio* — caused upheaval in the settlement. The remaining inhabitants — the more responsible had fled after the *Lexington* raid — assumed, because the flag had changed, everything had changed.

Onslow's instructions were to explain to any foreigners he found on the islands not only the relations in which they were to continue to hold themselves to the Crown of Great Britain, but also to allow them to continue undisturbed in their agricultural and other inoffensive employments. Which would have meant, had it been explained to them, their continuing as they were, as employees of Vernet. As the report of the *Tyne* captain makes clear, this was not done. The storekeeper and the *capitaz*[1] of gauchos, who had been left in charge of the settlement, intended, the captain reported, now that the islands had become British, to give immediate directions for the cattle to be destroyed so that they could personally benefit from the sale of the hides.

When the *Beagle*, on its surveying cruise, arrived three months later, Captain Fitzroy was appalled. Instead of the cheerful, little village he had expected, he found a few half-roofed stone cottages, some straggling huts of turf, staved-in boats, broken ground where a few cabbages and potatoes still grew, some sheep, goats, pigs, horses and cows, with here and there a miserable human being. The settlers seemed to think they were at liberty to do what they pleased with Vernet's private property as well as with the wild cattle and horses. Sealers swarmed everywhere.

The manner of the British arrival bears all the marks of instant reaction, a sudden take-over of territory

[1] The capitaz was the man in overall charge of the gauchos.

containing people regarded like the wild cattle as indigenous items and, from the reports, not dissimilarly feral. In the succeeding years, the British relationship with the islands was to be a series of instant reactions to sudden events. There was no policy as such. Even the decision, when it came, to colonise them could be described as one of sudden reaction.

In his report, Captain Onslow suggested, but not as a matter of urgency, that, in view of the numerous sealing vessels resorting to the islands, a small force should be permanently stationed at the port to preserve order and authority and to protect the settlers in their peaceful pursuits, and that the island be visited frequently by HM ships and vessels of war. A year later, a small force arrived but by then the damage had been done.

While the *Beagle* was in port Brisbane returned. Encouraged by the fact that the *Clio* had not only left him in full possession of his property but had entrusted his storekeeper with the care of the British flag, Vernet took this to mean that his settlement would be allowed to continue and, with the help of friends, had acquired the wherewithal to despatch Brisbane to restore the establishment.

Brisbane presented his papers to Fitzroy, who reported that he was quite satisfied with their tenor and the explanation he gave of his business, which was to act as private agent only to look after the remains of Vernet's private property. They had not, he added, the slightest reference to civil or military authority. He described Brisbane as an honest, industrious and most faithful man who feared no danger and despised hardship.

Fearlessness was what Brisbane was to need in the days that followed. He had trouble with the settlers, particularly the gauchos who, having roamed at will on Vernet's horses, killing cattle as they pleased and selling the beef to the numerous sealing vessels, did not take kindly to being regimented again. It was this, not the alleged payment by Brisbane to them in paper money instead of silver, as the British Government was to allege

on no other basis than gaucho gossip picked up by
visiting naval captains, that sparked off the gaucho
eruption which, on 26 August 1833, resulted in the deaths
of Brisbane, the storekeeper Dickson, the *capitaz* of
gauchos, an Argentinian and a German trader in a
massacre which became known as the Port Louis
Murders. The confusion arose because Vernet had his
own paper currency for use within the settlement, partly
for convenience, partly to prevent settlers being robbed
by rapacious shipmasters when they offered goods for
sale.

Brisbane's clerk, John Helsby, who himself narrowly
escaped assassination, recorded the events of 26 August
and the ordeals of the survivors during the following four
months during which time they were marooned on an
islet in the Sound. They were rescued with the arrival of
the *Challenger* on 9 January, bringing the first British
authority, its own First Officer, Lieutenant Henry Smith.
This seems to have been an ad hoc appointment following
an encounter with the *Hopeful,* a sealing vessel with a
naval lieutenant aboard, which had temporarily relieved
the marooned islanders at the end of October. Lieutenant
Smith and his accompanying boat crew of four had
volunteered to come.

Lieutenant Smith was a British authority in name only.
He came without instructions. He was not told what to
do, what not to do. He was provided with no funds, given
no ship. He was, however, officially installed, the
Challenger firing a salute of twenty guns. His precise
function is not clear. Throughout his stay he called
himself the Resident which, in the circumstances, was as
good a description as any.

The day after his installation, Lieutenant Smith and
twenty officers and marines from the *Challenger* started
off on foot into the interior on the hopeless task of
catching the mounted murderers. As guide, they took
with them one of the gang of eight assassins who had
turned King's Evidence. After twenty days, travelling
through incessant rain, they had to give up. So did the

captain of the *Challenger*. Deciding that catching murderers was a task he could afford to spend no more time on, he sailed off to get wrecked on the Patagonian coast. He left behind six marines to help Lieutenant Smith and his crew in their search. The murderers were not caught until March, just before the *Beagle* arrived on a second visit.

After capture, the ringleader, Rivero, was held aboard the *Beagle* in irons until a cutter arrived to take all the assassins to the flagship at Rio. From there they were taken to Sheerness. They were never brought to trial. The Law Officers of the Crown, while agreeing that the evidence was sufficient to warrant a conviction under the appropriate Act, deemed it inadvisable 'under the peculiar circumstances of the case' to carry the sentence, should there be a conviction, into execution. Accordingly, they recommended no prosecution. The Admiralty was instructed to 'dispose of the individuals', which it did by taking them back to Montevideo, where they stepped ashore free men.

The peculiar circumstances were that the murdered people were all employees of Vernet. To have brought a charge against their assassins would have entailed a recognition of his settlement and of his right to be on the islands.

If the treatment accorded the murderers by the British Government was surprising, that given Rivero, the ringleader, by the Argentine Government was even more so. Adulation was heaped on him. He became a national hero. The group who hijacked an Argentine airliner to Stanley in 1966 distributed leaflets intimating that Stanley, when their country took it over, would be renamed after him and, for a time after the Argentine invasion, it was. By some curious alchemy, Brisbane, whom Rivero personally took by surprise and killed, became transformed in Argentine eyes from his real status as a Vernet associate to a symbol of the Britain which 'seized' the islands in January 1833, though in that month he was with Vernet in Buenos Aires helping the

Buenos Aires Government in their wrangle with the US Government over the *Lexington* affair. In its Statement to the United Nations, Argentina links the murderers (not mentioned by name) to the indignation felt in Argentina after the *Clio* take-over. The removal of the assassins to England becomes, in her interpretation, 'the rest of the settlers who resisted the invaders were taken and sent to London for trial under different pretexts and never returned'.

Lieutenant Smith had been seven months on the islands before the Colonial Office became aware he was there. Then it wanted to withdraw him and his men because 'of the dire peril' in which they had been placed — news of the massacre had reached London just before — but was restrained by Lord Palmerston who pointed out that, in view of the discussions then going on with Buenos Aires — that country had lodged a Protest over the *Clio* affair in April 1833 — such action might bear the appearance of an abandonment of HM's claim.

On the islands, the still-uninstructed Lieutenant Smith, being a practical man, did what had to be done. He proceeded to put the Vernet establishment to rights, which meant, since he knew nothing about the management of cattle or the use of horses in procuring them, he strictly followed the methods Vernet had introduced. In regard to the settlers, he said later, he guided his conduct as if Mr Brisbane was still living. In so doing, he was not to endear himself to the authorities. When he returned to Britain after his four and a half years, and made himself available to the Colonial Secretary to give, as the first representative of the new British administration on the Falklands, a first-hand account of how things were there, he was refused an interview.

By then moves were well afoot to erase the Vernet connection from the islands. The process of disentanglement went on for years. It was to become a harrowing tale. On the one side was Vernet, so aware of and possessing real knowledge of the islands, desperate to return not just to continue his establishment but to develop the Falklands into what he could clearly see they could become: a great little country. On the other, a blinkered British administration, ignorant of the islands, caring less and politically fearful, which could not, until it was too late, separate Vernet from the Buenos Aires Government. This, despite all the information Parrish had made available to them while he was Consul General and his more recent personal recommendation that, if the islands were to be colonised, Vernet was the person to undertake it.

When eventually it soaked through that the uninstructed Lieutenant Smith was instructing himself by making a viable unit of the Vernet establishment, he was peremptorily informed he could not indulge in trade. When he passed management to his son, he was told he would still be responsible. Vernet was informed if he had property on the islands he should go there himself to manage it but, when he prepared to do so in the Vernet manner, by acquiring horses to take down to maintain the reserve he kept in training, he was told new settlers were not being admitted. Later, he was told, if he had any property on the islands, he must remove it; then told, if he went to the islands, he would be treated as a trespasser and forcibly removed. When eventually the Admiralty realised, as a result of Captain George Grey's report on his visit in 1836, that, without the horses and saddles belonging to Vernet, the 200 cattle feeding around the settlement, and essential for its existence, could not have been caught and tamed, and told the Colonial Office that, in their view, Vernet was deserving of substantial reparation, the Colonial Office did not agree. Vernet had been a trespasser on British rights and property. It was to the Buenos Aires republic he should look for indemnity, it being under their protection he had embarked on a speculation which brought his ruin. In any case, they did not know of any colony or body of men at the Falklands for whom it was necessary to purchase horses.

During the Rosas regime in Buenos Aires, Vernet was

debarred from making any contact with the British Government regarding his property on the islands. After the dictator's downfall, Vernet spent five years in London endeavouring to convince an even more intractable Government that the property it had taken over at the settlement was his and he should receive compensation for its confiscation. He was eventually awarded a token sum, based, as regards his horses, not on their arrival value in the islands but on what they had cost him before shipment. From this a deduction was made in respect of some of his paper currency which an islander possessed.

The Colonial Office was to carry its rejection of Vernet to extreme lengths. It was not sufficient to exclude him physically from the islands. His ideas about them had also to be excluded. When colonisation was eventually decided on, his memorandum on the islands (which he prepared for Parrish) was included with other reports sent to the Colonial Land and Emigration Commissioners when they were instructed to prepare a report on the best way to colonise the islands, but with a note appended that it was not to be pirated or quoted. The result was that his remarks on agriculture and climate, based on his personal observations, were discounted and his ideas on colonisation discarded.

The decision to colonise the islands was a sudden one. Up to a month before it was taken, the Colonial Office was assuring enquirers that the Government had no such intention. What brought matters to a head was a draft contract for the lease of sealing rocks which, in late 1839, Lieutenant John Tyssen, the officer in charge, made with a settler and forwarded to the Admiralty, who passed it to the Colonial Office. The latter, realising that, by confirming such a contract, they would be in effect establishing a colonial relationship with a settler before a colony was formed, decided — it appears to have been a personal decision of Lord John Russell — to form a colony.

The Commissioners produced a report in which the obvious reason for forming a colony in the Falklands —

the possession of the necessary assets in a geographical location ideally situated for their profitable exploitation (the basis on which Vernet had envisaged creating his thousand farms) — was excluded and the islands considered primarily from their locational value, as a place where merchant vessels could refit and the navy have a useful port of call between the Atlantic and the Pacific. Their one excellent suggestion, that a penal colony be set up on some of the more remote islands and convict labour employed in the necessary early construction work, was rejected by the Colonial Office. Their remarks on agriculture were to become enshrined as natural truths about the Falklands. On the assumption that the various settlements which had been on the islands during the last eighty years — which excluded the Vernet settlement as its experiences were irrelevant — would have thoroughly tried the capabilities of the soil, they concluded that the agricultural prospects were poor because 'there was still not one single tree growing' on the islands. This myth was to prevail despite the discovery two years later that in the indigenous tussac, up until then regarded solely as thatching grass, the islands had a 'tree-plant' of the highest nutritional value to livestock. The discovery was made by Joseph Hooker (later to become a famous Victorian botanist), who was assistant surgeon and botanist aboard the *Erebus,* the Antarctic exploring ship then wintering at Port Louis. So impressed was he with its qualities as well as its delightful appearance — a dense cluster of long evergreen leaves cascading palm-tree fashion out of a tall, thick, fibrous conical base — that he named it 'the golden glory of the Falklands'. It was to disappear from the main islands after the introduction of sheep as the economic unit.

The recommendations of the Commissioners on the course to be pursued in effecting settlement, which were to accompany the first governor to the islands as 'the rule for his guidance', put as first priority the selection of a principal port, the Admiralty having decided that Port William (where Stanley now is) would make a safer and more convenient main port of call then Berkeley Sound where the existing settlement was.

Richard Moody, who was to become first Governor, was a lieutenant in the Royal Engineers, 'Why an officer from the Engineers?', asked Fitzroy, now a Member of Parliament. It was a question Moody in due course was to ask himself.

In some respects, his situation was not unlike that of his predecessor, Lieutenant Smith. Like him, he was given no precise instructions. Lord John Russell informed Moody, in his letter of appointment, that his government was to be one of influence, persuasion and example rather than one of direct authority. He was given the courtesy title of Lieutenant-Governor though in the eyes of the Colonial Office he was considered 'not so much as a governor as an investigator who had to report the result of his enquiries and to state whether it would be prudent to found a colony or not'. For this purpose, however, he was provided with no ship, which was to hamper him in acquiring information about West Falkland as well as to cause problems when the decision was taken to move the settlement from Port Louis to Stanley.

Moody and his party, consisting of twelve Sappers and Miners, with their families — in all twenty-six people — sailed for the islands in October 1841. The Colonial Office would have preferred a smaller party and that made up of retired Sappers. Moody convinced them that, in a new country, non-retired Sappers would be of more use, a concept they were soon to dissociate themselves from, as, within a few years, they were to send as first settlers in Stanley, a group of Chelsea and Greenwich Pensioners.

Chapter 6

The British Colonisation

Two decisions, taken in the early 1840s, were to determine the Falklands' future — as a British backwater at the far end of the world. The first was the decision to move the settlement from its viable location in Port Louis to where Stanley now is. The other was to sell the islands' chief asset, its magnificent wild cattle, to a Montevidean cattle killer.

Moody rated the first of such priority that he did not wait to be formally inaugurated before he was off to have a look at Port William. Pleased with what he saw, he would have arranged to move there immediately had he not to make use of Lieutenant Tyssen's ketch, while it was still available, to carry out a more general inspection of the islands for the report he had been requested to prepare on their suitability for settlement. Bad weather cut short his tour, preventing a close look at West Falkland but at Port Howard he was able to get first-hand proof of the salubriousness of that island's climate when two seamen, brought aboard after living on it for fourteen months, were found, when medically examined, to be in excellent health.

He also encountered the survey team who for several seasons had been cruising around the islands preparing material for a nautical chart and found that their leader, Lieutenant Robinson, did not share his enthusiasm for Port William. In Robinson's view, it was not sufficiently capacious for the purpose intended. It was suitable only for a few vessels at a time calling on their passage or for vessels in distress unable or unwilling to beat up Berkeley Sound.

Moody decided to get a third opinion: that of, as he described him to London 'so distinguished an authority as Captain Ross', leader of the Antarctic Expedition.

When Moody revisited Port William with him in June (winter) 1842 he discovered that the surrounding ground was bogland. He told London no settlement should be undertaken until the land had been drained. It would be inadvisable to retard the growth of the colony and damp the ardour of newly-arrived settlers by requiring them to occupy a site entailing a great deal of labour and expenditure of capital at the beginning of their settlement. London already knew that the area was swampy. It had been told so by Lieutenant B. J. Sulivan, Robinson's predecessor on the nautical survey, when he had written specially to the Colonial Land Commissioners advising against the move.

Captain Ross came out firmly in favour of Port William. The Colonial Land Commissioners decided this was the definitive view and advised the Colonial Office accordingly. As they phrased it, 'the capital should be at whichever port should be decided by a competent authority to afford the greatest advantage to shipping and Captain Ross's report was clearly conclusive on this point.' Moody, who had in the meantime laid out a temporary capital at Port Louis and received the approval of the Colonial Secretary to name it Anson, was instructed to move forthwith. As for the outlay settlers would be required to make to drain the soil, this was no more than a necessary expense of colonisation, like that of clearing land of timber in other colonies.

The settlers, now numbering, excluding Moody's party, about fifty, were naturally reluctant to move. Moody was, he told London, the only person who did not view the prospect with disgust. The leading Anson citizen put it more bluntly. 'Of all the miserable bogholes in the Falklands Mr Moody has selected one of the worst for the site of the town.' A year later the Colonial Office, having discovered that not all naval authorities were unanimous about the superior advantages of Port William, instructed Moody to halt operations. But by then it was too late. Drains had been dug, the Sappers were building roads, Government House was taking shape. Most of the settlers had moved and were trying to establish themselves, as was Moody in his one bed-dining-reception-office. Stanley, named after the Colonial Secretary, officially came into being on 18 July 1845.

Moody provided London with further proof of the islands' suitability for instant settlement in the detailed report he prepared, based partly on his own brief tour but mainly on the observations of the naval surveyors and residents of long standing. More than half the land was good to excellent, he said, and could be put immediately to the plough. The poor land, about a quarter of the whole, was capable of rapid improvement. As it was, it could support two sheep to an acre (the present support over the entire islands is one to four acres). From the unproductive remainder, the settlers could obtain building materials and peat for fuel. Most of the bogs so lay they could be easily drained. Even the mountains were co-operative, not only providing pasturage to their tops but parting conveniently at places through which roads could be led. The immense beds of kelp ringing the islands would provide a plentiful supply of fertiliser. Only wood would have to be imported and that easily from the Strait region. So impressed were the Colonial Land Commissioners with the report that they asked permission of the Colonial Office to reprint parts of it when that Office decided to open up the islands for colonisation.

All hope of that went when, in January 1846, a contract was concluded with Samuel Fisher Lafone of Montevideo, giving him 'absolute possession and dominion over all wild cattle and wild stock whatever on the Falklands with full power to kill, sell or otherwise dispose of.'

Lafone was represented to Moody as a wealthy British merchant possessing funds and resources. In fact he and his brother Alexander, then operating from Liverpool, were being financed by a London firm of merchants. He was supposed to have become interested in the Falklands after Moody approached the British Consul in

Montevideo, who was his brother-in-law. His interest was, however, of long standing. In 1837 he had approached Vernet with the suggestion that they form a partnership to reinstate Vernet's concerns on the islands. A contract was drawn up but Lafone altered it so much in his own favour that Vernet could not accept. By then Lafone had learned all he wanted to know — the size of the large southern peninsula in East Falkland he was later to name Lafonia, where most of the cattle were, and all he needed to know regarding them. At the time he sent his representative to Port Louis 'to make certain enquiries relative to the nature of the pasture, climate and cattle', Lafone knew more about East Falkland than Moody did. Vernet had even supplied him with a map of the area the size of which he was later to dispute with the British Government.

Lafone was to be the first and most distinctive of the absentee landowners who were to become a characteristic feature of Falkland development in that he was absent from the moment he first expressed interest in the islands. He never set foot in them, not even when later he was appointed resident director of the Falkland Islands Company. His method was to operate through representatives and relatives. When difficulties arose he was therefore able to deny connection when need be.

This was to happen immediately the contract was signed. As no land survey had been carried out — none was to be until 1962 when there was an aerial survey for cadastral purposes only — it was agreed between Colonial Lands, who drew up the contract, and A. R. Lafone, who signed it on his brother's behalf, that the area he was to acquire for £60,000 (including wild stock over all the islands) should be described as 'that part of East Falkland whatever be its extent' lying south of what is now the Darwin isthmus, together with all the adjacent islands. Lafone seized on the publication of a new nautical map, which showed the area to be much less than on the map Moody and his representative had used in their discussions, to argue that the land allotted to him was much less than the 200 square leagues he had asked for and which he required to make the venture viable. His brother, he said, had signed the contract without his authority. When he found that the Government was willing to be amenable he then pointed out that, since the area allotted was less than what he had asked for, the number of cattle on it would be correspondingly fewer. He asked to be compensated for that. Also for the fact that the new issue of land, which the Government originally contemplated giving him, would be separated from his original holding entailing extra outlay on his part. Eventually, after nearly two years of haggling, the purchase price was halved, he was given more favourable terms regarding payment of instalments and excused from providing the Government with a specified number of tame animals each year, which Moody had hopes of making available to new settlers when they arrived but none of which were ever delivered as Lafone had from the start reneged on this requirement; as he did on most of the other clauses in the contract.

He used the Anglo-French blockade of Montevideo to get postponement of the shipment of a large number of sheep though he well knew, living in Montevideo, that the blockade was in fact a protective device to enable Montevidean merchants (mostly British and French) to carry on their businesses untroubled by the United Provinces-Banda Oriental dispute around it, which enabled trade to boom and Montevideo to become the commercial centre of the Plate. His manager also made use of the blockade to acquire from Moody his stock of hunting horses as well as his herd of tame cattle, thus making the settlement altogether dependent on him for its supply of beef. Under the contract the Lafone establishment was required to supply to the settlement beef of good quality and prepared for delivery in a proper manner, as in England. This stipulation was not heeded. Meat unfit for eating was frequently delivered. Often there was no delivery. On one occasion the settlers were reduced to petitioning the Governor for a schoooner to go to Port Louis to procure rabbits and geese. Lafone's manager, Williams, was equally cavalier in supplying others. In 1849 a letter appeared in the London *Times* on the unavailability of beef in the Falklands. The *Nautilus* had been unable to get a supply for its crew for a month. The letter also stated that the islands were in a distressed state.

The venture itself was a disaster. The cattle were ruthlessly hunted by semi-trained gauchos resulting in the deaths of thousands of calves as well as the destruction of most of the five hundred horses imported for the operation. Far from introducing the English settlers his representative had promised Moody, Lafone sent down what the first Governor described as foreigners of habits objectionable to an English community and his successor, George Rennie, as disorderly vagabonds. Lafone and his manager, he said, degraded a British colony to the barbarism of a province of the River Plate, Indians and Spaniards being thrown on the Government whenever it was inconvenient to employ them: the men had a verbal promise that their passage would be paid back to Montevideo at the expiry of their engagement but, when the time came, Williams would deny liability and the men would be turned loose in the settlement. Rennie was forced to introduce an Aliens Ordinance which Williams circumvented by landing his men at one of the harbours in Lafonia. In April 1849 Rennie shut the operation down for six months.

By the time it was due to be reopened Lafone had received his new contract and he and his brother were negotiating with their London creditors the launching of a joint stock company to take over their interests in the islands and busily distributing a 'Preliminary Prospectus of the Royal Falkland Land, Cattle, Seal and Whale Fishery Company', which was to become the Falkland Islands Company and assume the Lafone interests on 1 January 1851. The prospectus was later described by Lafone himself as 'too much gilded and highly coloured'.

The way of things introduced by Lafone continued

after his departure. Hunting down the wild cattle became
the colonising activity. Large acreages being necessary
for this, these became the norm of allotment. In the first
quarter century of British colonisation some 60,000 wild
cattle and 3000 wild horses were slaughtered in East
Falkland and about 20,000 cattle on West Falkland.
(They had been introduced there by one of the naval
lieutenants in charge of the settlement to provide settlers
with a stock of animals.) A governor at the end of the
century averred that most of the early settlers paid for
their land-holdings out of the proceeds of the sale of
hides.

Allotments of land continued to be made from the
nautical map by the simple method of 'marking',
outlining the areas required, then calculating their size in
nautical mileage and entering the figure in the Deed of
Title without prefixing 'nautical'. Landholders thus
acquired more land than they paid for. This free issue,
estimated at between 500,000 and 800,000 acres, was,
with the 'closed shop' manner of allotment whereby only
those with already large acreages were able to acquire
land when it became available, was to become a running
sore in the body politic of the islands. Steady acquisition
in this manner by the Falkland Islands Company (now
part of the Coalite Group) has resulted in its now owning
forty-three per cent of the islands. In recent years there
has been a slow move towards splitting up some farms
into smaller sections enabling more people to acquire
land.

The extractive style of farming — immediate
maximum gain for minimum outlay — continued when
sheep were introduced. The gauchos were replaced by
shepherds from Scotland but only in such numbers as
were necessary to provide a minimum labour force.
Minimum shepherding inevitably resulted in high sheep
loss. A. R. Wannop (1961) put the average flock
mortality at around ten to twelve per cent or 63,000 to
75,000 out of an approximate total sheep stock of
630,000. The average annual loss in lambs, he estimated,

at around thirty-five to forty per cent. The principle of minimum shepherding has been carried to its ultimate in recent years with the withdrawal of shepherds from their outside stations into the settlements and a reduction in Camp[1] employment generally. The advent of contract shearing has also helped to reduce the labour force on large estates and aided the rapid depopulation which has occurred in recent years.

Over the years minimum use has been made of carcass meat. A mutton-canning factory operated for nine years before and during the First World War. After the Second World War a freezer built by the Colonial Development Corporation functioned for about two years.

Further loss has ensued from what Munro, a New Zealand sheep expert, described in 1924 as the 'steady drawing on principal', continually taking from the pastures and putting nothing back. Deterioration of the pastures first became evident towards the end of the nineteenth century but for many years after, whenever nature became over-rebellious and financial loss seemed imminent, a war would intervene to shoot up the price of wool. The Boer War, the First and Second World Wars, and the Korean War have each played their part in the maintenance and financial growth of extractive sheep farming in the Falklands.

Down the years a steady stream of experts have visited, a steady stream of reports have been produced but it is only in the last twenty years that pasture improvement has really begun to make an impact on extractive farming consciousness. There have been one or two exceptions, particularly among the small island farmers who, over the years, have taken care of their pastures. A Grasslands Trial Unit, financed by the British Government, is now resident on the islands to help in what will be a long hard haul ahead.

Agriculture still remains an unregarded activity. As for the cattle, the source of all Falkland farming, the

[1] The Camp is the name given to the countryside in the Falklands. It derives from the Spanish word 'campo' and became current during the Vernet colonization.

Ministry of Overseas Development team who visited in 1971 discovered that farmers regarded them as a necessary evil from which milk, butter and an occasional bit of beef could be obtained. Few, they said, took them seriously as grassland improvers.

The only positive thing that was to result from the siting of the capital in its new situation was the practical proof it was to provide of Moody's assertion that bog could be turned into productive land. From the Stanley swamp the settlers were to create highly productive vegetable and fruit gardens despite the fact they were beset with drainage problems into the following century. They had to suffer two peat slips — when the liquid peat slid down from the heights above engulfing part of the town — much typhoid and dysentry before these problems were solved with the installation of main drainage in 1920.

The purpose-built capital never served the purposes for which it had been created. No steps were taken to make it a major port of refit. Nor did the Admiralty do anything about establishing it as a naval port of importance. It became for them merely a place to visit in the course of colonial duty.

During its first quarter century Stanley did become a minor port of repair for disabled shipping and, in the view of Sulivan, could have become the halfway port of the whole Australian and Pacific trade had it been provided with a patent slip for carrying out ship repairs. He reckoned that hundreds of vessels which then went into South American ports at ruinous expense would have come to Stanley. An attempt was made to get some of the £20,000, the initial and only payment received from Lafone, most of which had been earmarked for public works instead of immigration, as Moody had wished, allocated to the provision of a slip but London was not forthcoming. It was never to move far from the view that expenditure on the Falklands beyond the minimum was a gross extravagance. It did, however, speedily supply an establishment. By 1846 that comprised a governor —

Moody was made definitive in 1843 — chaplain, surgeon, magistrate, two clerks, harbour master, customs officer, jailer and surveyor.

A factor completely overlooked in the siting of Stanley on its nub of extruding land at the end of the islands was that such a situation with a range of hills intervening between it and its hinterland would not make for a natural connection, such as Port Louis had. Roads were not to figure in the Falkland scheme of things until the 1970s when the road to Darwin was commenced. The development of the interior of the two main islands into what were virtually large self-contained estates, each with its own harbour with always available water transport, made roads as far as the Camp was concerned, unnecessary. Until the construction of the road to the airport, the only roads Stanley had were some twelve miles radiating from the town, constructed as part of a Government plan to relieve unemployment during the 1930s Depression. When it ended so did they.

The geographical separation of the capital, Stanley, from the country was exacerbated in the early days by economic separation: Stanley with its ship-repairing industry having no need of the Camp; the Camp, in its activity, having no need of Stanley. A distinction that was to become a division began which was to endure until Argentina intruded into island life. The Falklands became a country of two parts, Stanley and the Camp, the people of Stanley versus the Campers, the working-class versus the Establishment, the under-privileged versus the over-privileged.

Stanley thus became, so far as it could under a colonial administration, a place of protest, but its efforts, directed primarily towards a more equitable distribution of land, required the help of a sympathetic governor to make impact. This it had towards the end of the nineteenth century when the original land leases fell in. Governor Sir Roger Goldsworthy made a strenuous effort to have the land surveyed and the surplus made available to the people of Stanley. London, however, overruled him.

Matters reached a head in the 1930s with the emergence of the curious phenomenon 'surplus population'. In the 1920s an enlightened governor had embarked on a comprehensive works scheme to improve Stanley, attracting labour from the Camp which was replaced by immigrant labour from overseas. When the Depression came the islands thus had a 'surplus population'. The Reform League, the first of only two democratic bodies to emerge in the Falklands, argued that there could be no surplus population in a land hardly developed and that those for whom no work could be found be put back on the land. Feelings ran high. There were acrimonious exchanges between Camp and Stanley. The Governor entered the fray, pointing out to the farmers that their loss in sheep, put at 85,000 a year, could be cut in half by putting the unemployed on to ditching and draining. Nothing was done. The problem was solved by the outbreak of war. The 'surplus population' found employment in the armed forces.

Throughout the British colonisation what has come to be called the islands' second industry, emigration, has been a distinctive feature of the Falklands. It began in ship-repairing days when the well-paid artisans could find no outlet for their earnings in the islands and has continued steadily down the years. The job opportunities for the indigenous Kelper — the name, originating in Stanley, at first meant a native of that town but after Argentina became a presence on the islands it came to mean any Falkland Islander — dwindled as the colonial system became established. Capable, intelligent, hard-working, he had to stand by and see expatriates, often of lesser ability, imported at great expense to do work which he, given training, could do equally well. There was only one outlet for the Kelper and that was to take himself and his family overseas. The exodus of islanders from the Falklands over the years could have repopulated the islands several times over. In recent years, particularly after the new Argentine connection, there has been a move, still small, to give the Kelper a greater say in the management of his affairs but there is still no Kelper doctor and only in recent years have any of the certificated teachers been of local origin.

It was not until after the Second World War, when universal suffrage was introduced at the insistence of Stanley, that the town acquired equal representation with the Camp on the Legislative Council. It is only in recent times that an indigenous Kelper, as distinct from a representative of the Camp and its allied mercantile interests resident in the town, has found a place on the Executive Council.

The basic needs of the town have always rated a low priority in colonial government thinking. The town still lacks a swimming-pool for which the foundation stone was laid in 1933. In 1947, thirty-three years after it applied for one, it got a town council, the last of the colonial capitals to get one and probably the first to have it taken away: in 1974, in the drive to incline the islanders towards Argentina, it was removed. It is still without the park for which the first Governor reserved 347 acres.

The second of the attempts to insert a degree of democracy into the colonial structure was the formation in 1964 of the National Progressive Party which described itself as the first political party, its aim to further the cause of progress in all things that concern the people of the Falklands, always bearing in mind the best interests and wishes of the people. Had it lasted beyond its one and a half years it could well have fulfilled a valuable function in educating the islanders politically. As it was, when the Argentine crisis broke they were in this respect to be largely naïve.

Chapter 7

The New Argentine Connection

I

The new Argentine connection began on 8 September 1964 when a small Cessna plane landed on the racecourse and the pilot, after planting the Argentine flag and handing a surprised Common Ranger[1] a letter, addressed to the Representative of the Occupying English Government, Islas Malvinas, took off before he could be apprehended.

The letter intimated that the pilot had descended into 'our national territory to ratify Argentine sovereignty in the archipelago'. His country, awakened from a long sleep and conscious of her moral and material grandeur, had resolved not to permit England to continue occupying an archipelago that for geographical, historical, political and just reasons belonged to Argentina.

His arrival coincided with the presentation of the formal Statement of Argentina's claim to the Falklands to the United Nations' Special Committee of Twenty-four on Decolonisation by her representative, Dr. Jose Maria Ruda.

The following year, despite strong objection from the United Kingdom delegate that the Committee was not competent to deal with the matter as it concerned a territorial claim not one of decolonisation, the Committee agreed, and the General Assembly subsequently resolved, in their Resolution 2065XX of 1965, that the 'Governments of Argentina and of the United Kingdom and Northern Ireland be invited to proceed without delay with the negotiations recommended by the Special Committee on the situation

[1] The Common Ranger was the man in overall charge of Stanley Common of which the racecourse formed part.

with regard to the implementation of the Declaration on the granting of independence to colonial countries and peoples with a view to finding a peaceful solution to the problem of the Falkland Islands (Malvinas) bearing in mind the provisions and objectives of the Charter of the United Nations and of Resolution 1514XV and the interests of the population of the Falkland Islands (Malvinas)'. Resolution 1514 was a general one recommending that colonial countries achieve independence.

In 1966 another, more spectacular, Argentine intrusion took place early on 28 September when a DC4 landed on the racecourse. The first islanders who went to have a look at the unusual visitor were met by men flourishing guns and hustled into the aircraft. The next-comers were handed leaflets intimating that the gunmen — and one gunwoman — had come to take over the islands on behalf of the country to which they rightfully belonged. The gunmen then ran up the Argentine flag and demanded to see the Governor.

The plane, belonging to Aerolineas Argentinas, had been on an internal flight from Buenos Aires to Rio Gallegos in southern Patagonia, with twenty-six passengers, when it had been hijacked and the pilot forced to divert to the Falklands. The hijackers, numbering twenty-one belonged to Condor, the youth section of Tacura, an extreme right-wing nationalist group. The purpose of the hijack was, in a year of internal historic significance — 1966 was the 150th anniversary of the formal Declaration of Independence from Spain of the United Provinces which became Argentina — to draw world attention, at the start of the United Nations' autumn session, to the Argentine claim to the Falklands.

The siege lasted a day and a half, during which the hijackers, taking advantage of permission granted the pilot to radio his whereabout to his employers, sent out a defiant message of No Surrender to their compatriots in Argentina. Then they succumbed to the cold and gave themselves up to the local cleric who had been acting as interpreter.

Two days later an Argentine transport arrived in Port William and took away not only the plane's passengers but the hijackers as well. At Ushuaia, capital of the southern province which, on Argentine maps, includes the Falklands, they were charged two months later not with the air piracy they had committed, and which the British Government, in releasing them for home trial, had demanded, but with carrying arms and depriving citizens of their freedom. The sentences were nominal — three years' imprisonment for the leaders, two years for the others. The rest got a suspended sentence of two years.

In Britain, where the existence of the Falklands was hardly known, the incident made headline news for a day and was then forgotten. In Argentina it was celebrated as a victory. Not only had Britain been seen to fall over backwards in her desire not to incommode Argentina but her handling of the situation — ordering the frigate HMS *Puma* from South Africa to the islands to remove the hijackers and then permitting them to leave on their own country's transport, allowing them to surrender to the local prelate and not to the Falkland authorities, housing them not in the prison but in an annexe to the Catholic Church, attended by priests not police — could have only one interpretation: passive endorsement of the Argentine view that the incident was an internal Argentine affair. The hijackers were heroes and two years later a plaque honouring their 'achievement' was unveiled in Buenos Aires.

A further aerial intrusion took place at the time of Lord Chalfont's visit in 1968 when the 1964 invader and one of the 1966 hijackers crash-landed outside Stanley. Again soft treatment was prescribed. They were returned to Buenos Aires on the ship which took Lord Chalfont there. Their plane was dismantled and shipped back.

After her initial Protest of 1833, Argentina's protesting against the British occupation had followed a desultory pattern. Sometimes an annual Protest would be presented. Sometimes, as between 1849 and 1884 and between 1888 and 1908, she would not bother to protest at all. In 1841 General Rosas offered to forego all Argentine claims to the islands if Britain would write off a London Loan. Britain refused to entertain the idea. In 1884, after she had completed her conquest of Indian Patagonia, Argentina added contiguity to her claim. Emotional attention to the islands began with the upsurge in nationalism generated by General Peron when he came to power in 1946 but, until 1964 there was only formal protest.

The passing of the UN Resolution quickly brought the British Labour Government to heel. In January 1966 Michael Stewart flew to Buenos Aires on the first-ever visit of a British Foreign Secretary to that country to have what was described as detailed discussions with the Argentine Government. On his return, he assured Parliament that sovereignty of the islands had not been discussed as the British Government did not regard this as negotiable.

On the islands rumour became rife but it was not until the following year, when the Governor, returning from 'routine talks' in London, informed the islanders that the British Government was being guided by a strong regard for their interests and would see there would be the fullest consultation with them, that they became concerned. The unofficial members of Executive Council expressed it in a letter they despatched in February 1968 to every British MP.

Then came the bombshell. On 28 March 1968 as dawn was breaking over the Houses of Parliament, Stewart disclosed to the few sleepy members still assembled that sovereignty of the Falklands was being discussed with Argentina.[1] The Government was firmly convinced, he

[1] According to a pamphlet entitled *Las Islas Argentinos del Atlantico Sur* compiled by the Jockey Club Argentino from material supplied by the Automobile Club of Buenos Aires and published in that city in 1982 after the invasion, the British Government was in fact at this time actively engaged in negotiating the transfer of the islands to Argentina.
    The ex-Argentine Ambassador to Britain, Brigadier Eduardo McLoughlin, is credited with stating that during his time in office confidential proceedings took place with a view to acceptance of

said, that sovereignty was legally British and had in consequence a clear duty to protect it but, equally firmly, Argentina was convinced of her claim 'and you had to allow sovereignty on to the agenda to continue good relations with Argentina'. He then proceeded to consider the possiblity of a transfer to Argentina of the sovereignty Britain had such a clear duty to protect. Not immediately. Only as part of an agreement assuring a permanently satisfactory relationship between the islanders and Argentina, in which there would be the fullest safeguards for the special rights of the islanders, the fact of their descent, their language, and so on. When questioned in the House of Lords about the holding of a referendum to ascertain islanders' views, Lord Chalfont, Minister of State at the Foreign and Commonwealth Office, replied that the Government was 'inclined to believe' the community was too small for a plebiscite to be necessary. In the House of Commons, Stewart was willing to admit a referendum but restrictively in relation to a possible future agreement with Argentina when the islanders' wishes would be prerequisite. On the situation generally they were, by implication, to be denied a voice.

Argentine sovereignty over the islands and that on 9 August 1968 after nearly two years of negotiations, both sides met at the Foreign Office and agreed that:

1. HMG would accept Argentine sovereignty of the islands from a date to be determined as soon as HMG was satisfied that the islanders' well-being would be taken into consideration by the Argentine Government.
2. Argentine sovereignty would be acknowledged after four and within ten years.
3. Future conversations would take place regarding arrangements to be made for the islanders' future.

The document was then presented to the British Government by Michael Stewart and to the Argentine Government by Dr. Nicanor Costa Mendez. The British cabinet approved the document on the understanding that a declaratory note would accompany its presentation to the UN signed by both parties. The wording of this was agreed by the end of October and a day and hour set for both Governments to announce the agreement.

In September 1968, however, the strict secrecy which it had been hoped to maintain was broken when a British newspaper got hold of 'some information' and published it.

Argentina took the view they had no right to one, because they were not a natural, indigenous people. They had been planted on the islands and had therefore none of the rights of a native people. What constituted a natural, indigenous people she did not define for the good reason no doubt that the manner in which her own indigenousness had been acquired did not bear looking into. A definition, however, was forthcoming from her mother country, Spain, whose claim to Gibraltar was then also before the United Nations. Gibraltarians, in Spain's view, could not be regarded as an indigenous people as they were not tillers of the soil and fishers of the sea, these being essential prerequisites for developing the necessary social and national characteristics from which a distinctive indigenous people could emerge. By the Spanish definition, the islanders were an indigenous people.

Stewart's allegation, in his speech, that the dispute, as it was henceforth to be described, was hampering communications between the islands and the mainland was rebutted by the Falkland Islands Emergency Committee, which came into being on 15 March 1968 when the slant of the Labour Government's intent had become evident. The islands, they said, were adequately served by their sea link with Montevideo and thence with Britain, their main source of supply. All they needed was an airstrip capable of taking commercial aircraft. The *Darwin* a vessel of some 700 tons, owned by a shipping subsidiary of the Falkland Islands Company and operating under Government subsidy, had been built in 1956 especially for the monthly Stanley-Montevideo run. It also provided passenger and cargo service around the islands after each trip to the mainland.

In November, Lord Chalfont, who had been accompanying the Queen on her South American tour (which had pointedly excluded the Falklands) arrived in the islands 'to put islanders' minds at ease regarding the British Government's intentions and the future of their homeland'. Instead, he succeeded in sowing seeds of

gloom and uncertainty. On West Falkland, where he
landed, he told his audience that, while they might not
wish for change, their children could well feel otherwise.
On East Falkland he concentrated on the economy,
helped by a swing to down in the wool price and a deficit
in the Colony's books, and feared for the future viability
of the islands. In Stanley, his audience was told it was
HMG's responsibility to look ahead and see what their
best interests would be in the next generation or after. A
statement which, had he dared make it in a black colony,
remarked one Kelper irately, would have earned him a
shot in the head.

Executive Council deliberations being secret, no
statement was forthcoming at the end of the four days.
Chalfont was closeted with a Council specially enlarged
for the occasion by the co-option onto it of the four
elected members of the Legislative Council. These elected
representatives were to remain part of the Executive
Council until the next election at the end of 1971. The
effect of their co-option was that during the vital period
when their own communications system was being
dismantled and their dependence on Argentina's
organised, the islanders were deprived not only of
information when they needed to be informed but also of
a voice.

Probing by visiting journalists revealed that Chalfont
had advised the Council that Britain was about to reach
an agreed position with Argentina compounded of two
parts. One would itemise ways in which communications
could be improved between the islands and Argentina.
The other would record the differences between Britain
and Argentina about the future of the islands. The
Council accepted Chalfont's assurances that the British
Government was acting in good faith and that the wishes
and interests of the islanders would remain paramount.
The press were less trusting. The British Government,
they reckoned, would proceed to set in motion a course of
events eventually to bring about the ceding of the islands
to Argentina.

Islanders' suspicions were temporarily allayed when they were told that officials of the Civil Aviation Department of the Board of Trade would be arriving the following year to carry out a feasibility study of the Cape Pembroke area as a potential site for the islands' own airport.

In June 1970, when the Council representatives arrived in London to take part, with British officials, in the first of three rounds of talks on Communications with Argentina, they were informed by the Falkland Islands Company that the *Darwin* was obsolete and uneconomic and would be withdrawn at the end of December 1971. The representatives were stunned as six months earlier the ship had been fit enough to receive a subsidy from the Government for a further two years. The news had, however, the natural — perhaps intended — result of making them more receptive to Argentina's offer of an air link. And it would seem to much else besides. When the islanders finally got details of the talks — which was not until nearly a year later, in May 1971, in a Government broadcast — they were amazed to learn that the talks, which the previous Governor had told them would be solely about communications, had been about practically everything, including their own exemption from Argentine military service. Also, that when travelling through Argentina, they would be unable to use their own passports. They would require a special document issued by Argentina.

The islanders were still reeling from the revelations when a British radio report from Argentina announced that the softening up of islanders preparatory to an Argentine take-over had begun. The Governor hastened to the microphone. He had not been appointed Governor and Commander-in-Chief of the islands to dispose of any part of the Queen's Realm, he said, but the British Government did wish to see a viable economy and this was becoming difficult without an economic pattern of external communications. In fact, within the year the economy had become viable without reference to any style of communications. The price of wool soared, balancing the Colony's books.

Seven months after their representatives had received the information the islanders learned, in a special broadcast by the Company's local manager, that the *Darwin* was to be withdrawn. Another five months elapsed before they knew that Argentina would be providing an air link. In the interval they learned they had a communications problem and that a two-man team from a well-known firm of London consultants would be arriving to solve it. The solution they recommended was a communications tie-up with Argentina.

The necessary documents to bring this about were initialled at the second round of Communications talks held in Buenos Aires on 1 July 1971. A month later they became an official Exchange of Notes which took the form of a Joint Statement on Communications — to become known as the Communications Agreement — and an exchange of letters intimating that nothing in the Statement would affect the position of the two Governments regarding territorial sovereignty of the islands. The islanders were presented with a *fait accompli* two months after the Governor had assured them that the London talks were exploratory. The third round of talks which were purely token, as by then there remained nothing of substance to talk about, took place in Stanley in November 1972 following the official opening of the temporary airstrip.

In the Joint Statement the Argentine Government undertook to provide a temporary service by amphibian aircraft but, within a fortnight of the Exchange of Notes, an Argentine Technical Mission was on the islands selecting a site for a temporary strip to take land planes. For the type of service envisaged, the Governor explained in a broadcast, the amphibian was not the most suitable of aircraft. The necessary exchange of Notes was quickly effected and the temporary airstrip, put in place by Argentine labour with islander help, was officially opened on 14 November 1972.

Eleven days after the initialling of the Joint Statement, on 12 July, the Foreign and Commonwealth Office issued a statement. The British Government whose responsibility it was under the Agreement to take the necessary measures to arrange for a regular shipping service for passengers, cargo and mail between the islands and the Argentine mainland would not, it said, be taking over the shipping service from the Falkland Islands Company which would continue to operate the external service for cargo, passengers and mail. The islanders had to wait until the following December before they learned, by inference, from a radio programme, *Visitors Book,* in which the London chairman of the Falkland Islands Company was interviewed, that the shipping service which would be provided would not be passenger-carrying.

There would be two new ships, the chairman said, one a modern cargo vessel to replace the existing chartered seasonal wool-carrying one, the other a cargo ship for inter-islands trade. It was left to the islanders to deduce that a modern cargo vessel would not be passenger-carrying. On the new local ship they were informed more specifically. It would have cabin accommodation — for two stevedores. Shortly after they learned that the Government-owned inter-islands *Forrest,* which had cabin accommodation, would also not be available to them. It would be transferred to the Ministry of Defence for use of the British marines stationed on the islands to replace the hovercraft the ᵗ had used hitherto. In future, the islanders would have to do all their travel within the islands on the Government-owned seaplane.

With the inauguration in January 1972 of the amphibian air service between Commodoro Rivadavia on the Patagonian coast and Stanley, the islanders ceased travel-wise to be a sea-going people. After April, when LADE[1] the civilian wing of the Argentine Air Force, set up office in Stanley, they became dependent on Argentina to get off and on their own islands with the

[1] Lineas Aereas del Estados

introduction of the Certificado Provisorio (White Card).
This, the documentation Britain had devised with
Argentina to 'facilitate' the passage of islanders through
Argentina, became in practice a foreign pass without
possession of which they were marooned on their own
islands.

II

In 1972 a start was made on demolishing the colonial
pieces, the most important being the Falkland Islands
Company which was taken over by one of the Slater
Walker subsidiaries and, after two further takeovers, was
to cease to be the potent power it had been in the islands.
The European Space Research Organisation closed down
its tracking station on the outskirts of Stanley — for
technical reasons. The British Antarctic Survey would, it
was announced, be transferring its sub-Antarctic HQ
from Stanley to Cambridge, England — for economy
reasons. The Colonial Secretary became a Chief
Secretary.

Argentina, however, remained dissatisfied. Reporting
to the Security Council in Panama in March 1973, she
accused Britain of endeavouring to nullify the essence of
their meetings and threatened to 'change her position'. In
a letter to the Secretary General in August, she accused
Britain of virtually paralysing negotiations by
endeavouring to downgrade them to the level of talks
about air and sea communications and to avoid real
discussions about a transfer of sovereignty. In November
she threatened to roll up the airstrip if these were not
forthcoming, then changed her mind and, on the
anniversary of the opening, staged an impressive party,
forty-five Argentine VIP's attending including the Chief
of Staff of the Air Force.

Like Argentina of 1964, the islanders by now were
waking from their long sleep. The immediate cause was
the humiliating white card. A series of events also helped.
In quick succession they had the departure of the *Darwin,*

the ship that had served them so well, coinciding with the biggest pile-up ever of sea mail at Commodoro Rivadavia; a Government announcement that a contract was being negotiated with Yacimentos Petroliferos Fiscales (Y.P.F.), the Argentine State Oil Company, to build and operate a bulk storage plant in Stanley for the monopoly supply of petrol and oil; and a Secretariat statement that there was virtually no demand for a passenger and freight sea service to supplement existing transport arrangements and that the 1971 Buenos Aires Agreement was out of date on the subject.

They began to see the experts who, since 1972, had been arriving in increasing numbers to report on everything reportable-on, not as an aid to their betterment but as fulfilling a diversionary role. They grew wary of everything. Politically-orientated letters began to appear in the monthly *Review,* until then mainly a gossip sheet, which also adopted a political slant. The Falkland Islands Committee, which had replaced the Emergency Committee, set up a local branch. In the Legislative Council a motion objecting strongly to any negotiations or talks being held with the Argentine Government concerned in any way with transfer of sovereignty was defeated only on the Governor's casting vote. When, after a long delay, the British Government finally confirmed that the permanent airfield would be built, they requested, in their motion of thanks, that the runway be lengthened to take international planes. The islanders' greatest success was securing the appointment of a select committee of the elected members of the Legislative Council to review the Constitution. A long delay, however, attributed by the local *Times* (successor to the *Review*) to Argentine pressure on the British Government, ensued before the approval of the Privy Council to their recommendations was forthcoming.

Argentina countered all this with a deluge of good deeds. She laid on free flights for farmers to visit an agricultural show and *estancias* (cattle farms) in Tierra del Fuego and for school children to visit the Y.P.F.

plant. Argentine sailing clubs made donations of sailing craft to Stanley youth. The Government provided teachers to teach Spanish in Stanley schools. Children going to school in Argentina, on scholarships provided by Argentina, were presented with a post office savings book carrying free life insurance benefit and with books of poems by a leading Argentine poet. A comprehensive arts and crafts exhibition was staged in Stanley. There were offers of exchange family holidays for children.

She had already ensured in the October 1972 Agreement that LADE would be responsible for the regular air service when the airfield became operative. After the Oil Agreement was signed on 13 September 1974 she began to build a tank farm on the islands 'large enough to fuel the Argentine navy'. When, later, she decided to build a jetty to the oil storage plant she was successful in getting the British Government to foot the bill though, under the Agreement, this was her responsibility. In fact this jetty was never built.

Throughout she maintained her outside pressure. The delegates at the Inter-Parliamentary Union in London on 9 September 1975 were reminded of Britain's 'act of international piracy' in establishing a colony in the Falklands. Falkland Islanders in London picketed these proceedings.

The following month it was announced in London that an economic mission, headed by Lord Shackleton, and comprising oil, fisheries, finance and animal-husbandry experts, as well as a sociologist, would be going to the islands to carry out an all-embracing survey.

Why such a mission should be decided on at this particular juncture was not immediately apparent. The islanders, forgetful of past experiences, saw in its appointment (though it was not designated an official mission) a change of heart on the part of the British Government which seemed at last to have become mindful of their needs. It was to emerge that sending the mission was part of another convoluted re-orientating exercise (the first being the operation mounted to switch the islanders from their own transport to dependence on Argentina's) to encourage them into the Argentine fold by way of natural association in an economic tie-up between Britain and Argentina to develop the oil and fish riches offshore.

The possible presence of oil in the seas between the Falklands and Argentina had, in recent years, been attracting growing attention. A survey carried out by the University of Birmingham's geology department in 1974 had revealed promising hydrocarbon deposits. US geophysical surveys had proved even more optimistic. Oil companies were becoming keen to explore. Off the Argentine coast some had already begun. That the fish resources in the seas around were immense had been known for years. East European countries had been fishing advantageously between the islands and South Georgia since 1966.

In May 1975 a Council's delegation journeyed to Rio to be informed by Under Secretary Ted Rowlands of the likelihood of change in the islanders' lives should oil be discovered and exploited off their shores. They were also told that, without extra justification, he could not agree to present a case in Parliament for lengthening the runway, then under construction, to take international planes.

The display of tantrums Argentina was to mount when the Shackleton mission set out for the islands at the beginning of January 1976 denying it passage through Argentina so that the last lap of their journey had to be made in the *Endurance* and the first lap of the return, at the end of January, in the Royal Navy Auxiliary *Tide Surge;* requesting the withdrawal of the British Ambassador; creating several incidents, the most serious occurring after the mission had returned to Britain when an Argentine destroyer fired across the bow of the research ship *Shackleton* because it was 'in Argentine waters' — would appear to have been staged primarily for domestic consumption as Argentina had, through its representative at the UN, been made aware of the mission and its purpose the previous September and had raised no objection. It had also, in November, received what was in effect a 'mini-mission' when two MPs, one an oil expert, travelling under the auspices of the Commonwealth Parliamentary Association, had wide-ranging discussions with senior Argentine officials in Buenos Aires after spending three weeks in the islands covering every aspect of life — political, social, economic. It knew that to have included Argentines on the mission — the reason later given for her display of anger — would have rendered it unacceptable to the islanders. The Argentine authorities were also well aware that their people, accustomed to seeing their country in the driving seat in all matters concerning the Falklands, would not take kindly to what looked like a sudden brush off. The only way to demonstrate Argentina's importance in the situation was to lay on an impressive display of displeasure.

If the islanders were perturbed by a sudden dusk landing of what looked like invading troops but turned out to be fifty army engineers come, with their equipment, without prior permission from the Falkland authorities, to extend the temporary airstrip, though the permanent one was then on the point of completion, the Foreign Office was not. It followed, it said, from the 1972 Agreement. Nor in the House of Commons was James Callaghan. The Government recognised, he said, that the long-term interests of the islands must lie in practical forms of association with the Argentine mainland. This was to be echoed by the Governor at the meeting of the Legislative Council immediately prior to the publication of the Shackleton Report. The security and prosperity of this British Crown Colony could best be achieved, he said, by an evolving, harmonious and profitable relationship with their great neighbour on the South American continent.

Two days after the incident involving the *Shackleton* it was announced from Buenos Aires that the ship was to be withdrawn. The decision had been taken at a meeting in

New York between the Argentine Foreign Minister and Rowlands. The Foreign Office issued a prompt denial. What the two had talked about were ways of resuming the dialogue on the islands. Both versions proved correct. The *Shackleton* sailed off on February 20 never to return to the islands. Dialogue was resumed, to be followed immediately after the presentation of the mission's report to Parliament, by a spate of formal talks.

The report, which appeared in July, in two volumes, of nearly 500 pages, demonstrated in detail the state of stagnation and degeneration on the islands and the alluring prospects offshore. It counselled cautious speed in regard to the oil. More exploration would be needed before that resource could be adequately assessed. It made the point that oil companies would require political stability in the areas they sought to make exploration in.

Argentina, on her side, suffered no such inhibitions, offering for exploration and development in subsequent years areas that abutted ever closer into Falkland waters until eventually, in May 1981, the Foreign Office was forced to take the unprecedented step of inserting a notice, in the form of an advertisement in the *International Herald Tribune* politely warning the oil companies off.

Surprisingly, in regard to the fisheries, the value of which a proliferating number of foreign fishing vessels engaged in the area gave continuing proof, the mission recommended a look-see approach. It suggested that the White Fish Authority be invited to conduct an exploratory fishing survey, using chartered commercial fishing vessels to see if a potential fishery existed. It was not until after much prodding by the South Atlantic Fisheries Committee, formed in 1978 as an offshoot of FIRADA, the Falkland Islands Research and Development Association Limited, itself an offshoot of the Falkland Islands Committee, that any action resulted. Then it took the form of the commission of a Desk Study by the Ministry of Agriculture and Fisheries by the White Fish Authority into 'the fisheries potential

of the South Atlantic'. The Ministry of Overseas
Development also moved fractionally. They decided on
the appointment of a team of experts to examine the
possibility of coastal fishing and salmon ranching in the
islands.

Presented to the Foreign and Commonwealth Office in
December 1979, the Desk Study was not published until
April the following year after which, despite continuing
efforts on the part of the South Atlantic Fisheries
Committee to get action, nothing happened. By then
West German trawlers were catching and processing
hake from the waters around the islands for sale in
Europe. In 1979, 150 Comecon vessels visited Stanley.

Predictably high on the mission's list of island
shortcomings was the length of the runway which, if not
extended would inhibit development of tourism and
other diversifying potential. The islands would be unable
to become the headquarters of any fishing industry.

It was a sentiment echoed by Alginate Industries, a
British company engaged in the processing of alginates,
emulsifying agents derived from seaweed, widely used in
the food and other industries. Impressed by the immense
beds of kelp around the islands — they described the
Falklands as possessing the greatest stock of seaweed in
the world — they had, in 1972, set up a pilot plant in
Stanley and had hopes of establishing a factory for full-
scale production. Requiring political stability before they
could embark on such an enterprise, they sought but were
unable to get from the British Government an assurance
of continued British sovereignty of the islands. The
political climate, they said in their 1976 Report, seemed
to be changing for the worse. Government seemed to
have decided not to undertake any development which
did not have the approval of Argentina. In 1977 they
ceased operations in the islands. At the June Legislative
Council meeting the Chief Secretary gave as the reasons
doubts about the demand for kelp, island costs and the
outlook for world trade. Sovereignty was included under
'other factors'. A month earlier Alginate had announced
record profits of over £2m.

The emphasis in the Shackleton Report on the need to lengthen the runway was, for the islanders, its most important feature. The Government, however, reminded them in a broadcast commentary of the 'wider political and financial considerations, including the framework for co-operation with Argentina'.

The impact of the Report was to be overshadowed almost immediately by an impact of a more personal kind, a plane accident resulting in the death of a popular Kelper pilot under apparently mysterious circumstances and the reluctance of the Government to hold an independent inquiry which was to result in two members of Executive Council walking out of an emergency meeting and the use of the radio telephone to rouse the islanders to the situation, from which came the first-ever public demonstration held in the Falklands, over two hundred people taking part. The British Government, sensing an alarming development, acted with alacrity. Within days a Board of Trade investigating team was on its way to the islands. The Governor was replaced.

The reception accorded the Report in Argentina — the Government had been sent a copy on publication — was outwardly one of disinterest. The essential issue to solve, said an Argentine Foreign Ministry statement, was the dispute on sovereignty and they had no comment to make on matters not directly related with that. Their Minister of Economy, Sr Martinez de Hoz, in London to negotiate a loan, approved the idea of Britain and Argentina working together on the development of offshore resources such as oil. A year later, the Foreign Ministry had changed its tune. The Argentine Government, it said in an issued statement, would pressurise and prevent any company from exploiting marine resources around the islands unless done in co-operation with Argentina.

After digesting the Report for seven months the British Government revealed to the House of Commons on 2 February 1977 the result — talks with Argentina would be resumed immediately. Using the now familiar phraseology, Foreign Secretary Anthony Crosland told

the House that new developments in the Falkland
economy would require the framework of greater
political and economic co-operation in the region as a
whole. He did not, however, in this connection, see any
reason for extending the runway. At the appropriate
moment he would commission essential preliminary
studies to determine whether this was likely to be
practicable and cost effective. Mid-month, Under
Secretary of State, Ted Rowlands, was on his way to
Buenos Aires for three days of talks and, sandwiched in
between the first and final two, a five-day visit to the
islands.

III

The first intimation that the new series of talks would
take the form of negotiations was given to journalists by
the Argentine Foreign Minister, Admiral Guzetti, at the
end of the first day of talks when Rowlands was
journeying to the Falklands. On his return to
Commodoro Rivadavia, Rowlands revealed that the
British Government had gone the whole way to meet
Argentine insistence that, from then on, discussion on the
islands would include discussion on sovereignty. He
handed the reporters travelling with him a statement that
sovereignty would be discussed in formal negotiations
between the two countries, and expressing the British
Government's willingness to do so. While he was on the
islands he had made no mention of this. When asked by
the Goose Green branch of the Falkland Islands
Committee if he had discussed sovereignty with
Argentina on the way to the islands he refrained, in
assuring them he had not, from saying he would be doing
so on his return. He assured the Councils — Legislative
Council had again agreed to a joint association with the
Executive Council — that the British Government would
try to establish a basis for negotiations. He did not add
'on sovereignty'.

These exploratory talks were so successful — on the

Argentina side especially so, as the Dependencies of South Georgia and South Sandwich Islands were included in the sovereignty consideration — that Foreign Secretary, Dr. David Owen, was able to inform the House of Commons on 27 April that the next series of talks would concern future political relations including sovereignty and economic co-operation in all three areas as well as in the south-west Atlantic in general.

The first round took place in Rome in July and was followed in December by a further round in New York which set up two working groups, one to look into sovereignty, the other into co-operation in offshore resources. The third round of talks in Lima in February 1978, which included discussion on the constitutional future of the Falklands, came to a disagreeing end with the Argentine delegation walking out. The two sides did not meet again formally until December in Geneva. At these talks agreement was reached in principle on the outline of a scheme of co-operation in their scientific research activities in the Islands Dependencies. An Argentine source said afterwards this constituted the first step towards affirming Argentina's presence in the region.

She had been in the region since 1976 on South Thule Island in the South Sandwich group but the research station she had set up there was not discovered until November 1977 when the research ship *Bransfield* sighted it. The British press, anticipating another incident, got very excited. In the House of Commons Rowlands was less perturbed. When asked what HMG proposed to do he replied that it would continue to leave Argentina in no doubt of 'our position'. Later, in the House of Lords the Government spokesman admitted that the scientific co-operation proposals agreed to at the talks would legitimise the illegal occupation. There the matter rested. The Argentines continued to occupy South Thule until ejected by the British military in 1982.

Argentina reacted to the 'discovery' of their South Thule station by staging another incident in the islands.

Around the first anniversary of the opening of the
permanent airfield — it had been opened on 1 May 1977
by a non controversial figure, Sir Vivian Fuchs — LADE
announced that it would be carrying out a test flight of a
new jet F28 which it proposed to put on the Stanley run.
While this was taking place another plane appeared,
causing confusion, said the Falkland *Times,* one plane
being taken for the other. This plane flew low over two
Polish ships in Berkeley Sound, harrying them. The same
day, sixty-three miles north of the Falklands, a Polish
trawler was approached by an Argentine destroyer with
guns traversing, and ordered to heave to. It was boarded
by an Argentine officer who informed the Master he was
fishing in Argentine territorial waters. When the
Government was asked in the House of Commons about
the violation of Falkland waters and airspace, their
spokesman replied that an Argentinian naval aircraft had
intercepted Polish fishing trawlers claiming they were in
Argentine waters. They were outside the three-mile
territorial Falkland area. Berkeley Sound, for purposes
of the reply, had been moved out to sea.

In 1979 Britain had a change of government. A new
Under Secretary of State, Nicholas Ridley, assured the
House of Commons that dialogue with Argentina would
be continued in a constructive spirit. In July, on a
'familiarisation visit' to the Falklands, he assured the
islanders nothing would be done without their approval.
He did, however, tell them that it was more important to
settle 'this dispute' than to let it run on. He had detected
— he did not say where — a very strong desire for 'us'
(one of the changes in language affected by the new
Administration was the adoption of the more agreeable
first pronoun plural in place of 'British Government') to
try and improve relations with the Argentines. He
strongly urged islanders to take a robust view about the
need to involve Argentina in a lot of their activities on the
islands. It would be to their (the islanders') benefit. After
his call at Buenos Aires it was announced that diplomatic
relations between Argentina and Britain would be
restored to ambassadorial level.

At the United Nations in September, the Foreign Secretary, Lord Carrington, and the Argentine Foreign Minister agreed, in private talks, to proceed with negotiations on 'the future sovereignty and economic status of the Falklands'. In his speech later to the Assembly, the latter reiterated his Government's firm decision to persevere in the search for a prompt and just solution to 'this problem'. Milder words than Argentina's representatives had used hitherto.

Concurrent with the September meeting of the diplomats, diplomacy on a lower level was being practised down south. A group of islanders, lured to Palermo by promise of horses at £1 each made by a visiting vet, were being given VIP treatment, staying in luxury hotels, being loaded with gifts and granted the freedom of the City of Palermo, the key of which was accepted, on behalf of the Falkland visitors, by an expatriate Scotsman.

Before the first round of talks between the new British Government and Argentina in New York in April 1980 an Argentine Ministry spokesman expressed that country's intent: 'We want sovereignty to be transferred, together with a happy and integrated community, within a reasonable time.'

The talks between Ridley and his Argentine counterpart, Air Commodore Carlos Cavandoli, were described as exploratory, exchanges cordial, each side able to reach a better understanding of the other's position. One Islands councillor attended — the first time since the Communications Talks that there had been Falklands representation. 'Consultation with the islanders' during the series of talks held in 1977 and 1978 had taken the form of meetings in Rio between Rowlands and a Councils delegation, one held at the end of 1977, the other at the beginning of 1979. This procedure would appear to have been not unconnected with a statement put out in September 1977 by the Argentine Foreign Minister that his Government would not permit Falkland Islanders to participate in its talks with Britain over the future. Talks were strictly bilateral in accordance with the terms of the UN Resolution and should take into consideration their interests but not necessarily their desires.

Much to their surprise, Ridley was back among the islanders again in November 1980. They wondered why he had returned so soon. If they had listened a week earlier to the BBC World News they might have got a clue. The Argentine Foreign Minister, it reported, agreed with his British counterpart that there had been a significant improvement in Anglo-Argentine relations. Relations had improved in many fields, including talks on the sovereignty of the Falkland Islands. The UN had postponed a debate on the issue and agreed to delay further action on the future of the islands until the following year. Which could mean only one thing. The British Government had become amenable to an Argentine take-over of the islands. Ridley's speedy return was to arrange the manner of the hand-over.

Helpful in this direction would be the British Nationality Bill then making its way through Parliament. If it became law, one-third of the islanders would, lacking patrial connection, cease to have the right they had had of entering Britain as the Britishers they thought they were. The Labour members on the Standing Committee were to ensure it did become law by opposing an amendment which would have given the islanders full British citizenship, on the grounds that it would have a major effect on the relationship with Argentina and would undermine the possibility of stability for the islanders and a *modus vivendi* with Argentina in the future.

Ridley told the islanders he had thought it right to come and discuss with the people — starting with councillors, then moving to the Camp and to everybody — what they would like 'us' to do at the next round of negotiations. There were different options he would tell them about. He emphasised that he was not putting forward plans which the islanders should decide on. These were possiblities for negotiating positions. He did not know whether they would be acceptable to the Argentines until 'we' had had a chance to negotiate. It was impossible to say what firm proposals 'we' might then be able to come up with but the islanders could rest assured they would be laid before the people of the Falklands for them to decide on.

Ridley listed three options: a Condominium/Joint Administration; a Moratorium or Freezing of the dispute for a specified number of years; and a Lease Back scheme whereby Britain would hand over titular sovereignty to Argentina and then take out a very long lease on the islands.

The first he dismissed as a non-starter. He disapproved of it. He was sure the islanders would disapprove of it. It would seem to have been included to blur the fact that what the islanders were being presented with was a straight-forward choice.

Ridley did not say he disapproved of a Freeze. He focussed instead on the problems which would arise when the Freeze came to an end, the uncertainty there would be while it was in operation. There would also be difficulties regarding exploitation of the offshore oil and fish. He discountenanced any possibility of change in the islands during the period by not mentioning it. He also omitted to say that, under the Freeze, the islanders would retain the sovercignty of their homeland and thus their own national identity.

Under a Lease Back, he said, the prospects were limitless. It would unlock the great resources 'we all know' the Falklands have, both in sea and on land. He cited tourism, investment in hotels, improvement of farming, wool, meat exports, inshore fishing, deep-sea fishing — the islands would have a 200-miles maritime zone — licensing of foreign fishing, exploring for oil and gas. All of these, he told them, under a Lease Back would actually happen. There was the small matter of arranging a suitable period of lease. Argentina would naturally want it to be for the shortest time, 'we' for the longest. For a generation at least 'we' would demand, possibly for two.

He mentioned none of the drawbacks. That was left to
a member of the Executive Council who went on radio to
tell the islanders why they should not consider what he
described as the most serious attack on their liberties ever
mounted. To accede to a Lease Back would be to give
away the only important bargaining card they had. They
would be living in a rented country. The official advice
they were being given was slanted. The Minister, the
Governor, his assistant and the Foreign and
Commonwealth Office advisers accompanying Ridley
were all controlled people. They had to do what they were
told. The islanders should be careful not to accept any
solution which they offered which would give away their
sovereignty.

It was the nearest thing to a revolutionary speech the
islanders had ever heard but it touched a chord in them
that they, the Kelpers, were being denied the right to be
an indigenous people in the land of their birth. Ridley had
steered clear of mentioning their right to be decolonised
as a colonial people.

He was given an abusive send-off to the
accompaniment of *Rule Britannia*. He also got a drubbing
when he returned to the House of Commons.

If, like Chalfont before him, the object of his visit had
been to create divisiveness, he succeeded. The people,
families, were split. He was unsuccessful, however, in
obtaining a majority in favour of Lease Back. The
Legislative Council, when the matter came before it, in
January 1981, voted for a Freeze for twenty-five years, a
decision the two Councils representatives took with them
to the talks held in New York the following month.
Ridley, however, phrased it then less starkly. He
suggested a moratorium while the two nations worked
out joint fishing and oil exploration ventures.

The Argentine deputy Foreign Minister utterly
rejected the idea. He did, however, decide to talk
personally with the Falkland representatives — a day was
set aside for the purpose — on the subject of ceding
sovereignty. He asked them, presuming they agreed to

cede sovereignty, what the islanders would want. Would they draw up a list of their requirements. The delegates detailed their national differences — their whole way of life, customs, education, legal system, government, was different. All these things, he assured them, could be guaranteed 'for some considerable time'. The only thing Argentina wanted was sovereignty of the islands.

At the end of the meeting a brief statement, replacing the communiqué, which the Argentine delegation requested be withheld, was issued agreeing to further negotiations, dates for which were to be arranged after the new Legislative Council had been elected in November.

This new Council, according to a statement made by the representatives on their return to Stanley, would decide whether to accept some form of Argentine sovereignty or to drop out of the negotiations. No decision, however, was taken at its first meeting on 5 November. The matter, it appears, was not discussed. The two delegates who went to New York on 25 February 1982 for the postponed talks — they had been postponed from December at Argentina's request — took with them no mandate from the Legislative Council. They were, as island representatives had been prior to the 1981 talks, merely 'attendees'.

The Ridley proposals now buried, the situation was back as before. The position Argentina intended to take at future talks was made plain in a Note sent to the British Ambassador in Buenos Aires which was reproduced in the September Falkland *Times* — the first time ever any such exchange had been published locally. In the Note the British Government was requested to give 'resolute impetus' to the formal process of negotiating intended to solve in conclusive manner — by which she meant in her favour — Argentina's claim to the Malvinas, South Georgia and South Sandwich Islands. Despite the close — at times over-close — contact the islanders had had with Argentina during the past nine years, the Note said that the ignorance the islanders suffered from in regard to that country, due to the isolation in which they lived, was the real obstacle preventing the advance of the negotiating process, 'as wishes rather than interests could be put forward as a permanent argument to obstruct progress'. 'With all due respect for islanders', the matter was a bi-lateral one between Britain and Argentina. There were in practice only two alternatives: effective Argentine sovereignty or continuation of the present colonial state of affairs. So far as Argentine policy was concerned, an acceleration of negotiations with a clear objective in view had become an unpostponable priority. The time had come for negotiations to become effective.

In accordance with this, her delegates at the talks recommended that a negotiating commission be set up to discuss all outstanding questions of sovereignty, trade and development. It should meet monthly, preferably at Ministerial level and be committed to reach a conclusion by the end of 1982, in time, that is, for Argentina to be able, in the following January, on the 150th anniversary of the 'seizure' of the islands by the British, to lay on a celebration commemorating their 'liberation'.

Richard Luce, who had replaced Ridley as Under Secretary of State, agreed to the setting up of such a commission but wanted a longer period for negotiating. He was now faced with a real difficulty — how to induce into the Argentine fold the people who, a year before, had rejected any close connection.

The news the Argentine representatives took home from the talks did not augur well for the Government's plans. In Luce's desire to lengthen the negotiating period, it saw yet another attempt on the British side to protract proceedings. It could not conceive that this time the British had a real problem because it could not conceive that the islanders were real people. So long accustomed to regarding them as political irrelevancies in what, to them, was purely a bi-lateral problem, it was incapable of realising that they, like its own people, could have a physical and emotional affinity with the land of their birth as deep-seated and as abiding.

Succeeding British Governments had encouraged Argentina in this belief by their own negative attitude towards the islanders, regarding them as 'adjacent difficulties' to the 'problem' and islander opposition to Argentina as intransigence, something to be overcome. They failed to see — or cared not to — that this intransigence came out of the islanders' lack of basic liberties. The colonial system, under which they were forced to live, denying them natural self-expression, had bred in them a deep frustration which was compounded when an unasked-for Argentine connection was foisted on them, followed by their never being allowed to know what was supposedly being done on their behalf. 'Consultation with the islanders' meant informing Council delegates, one of whom was always a member of the Executive Council, which ensured that all such information proceeded no further. Resentment consequently mounted and became targeted on the very people the British Governments were so anxious to connect them with. Argentines became Argies, a term of dislike.

Because the islander numbers were small, British Governments tended to assume that their requirements were equally diminutive, not least in their need to be decolonised. These Governments, which could readily see the need for decolonisation when people of different colours were involved, failed to notice that the same need could exist when both sides were of identical colour or that size of numbers did not change the facts of colonial subjugation. It did not occur to them that people held in colonial bondage could be induced into a relationship with another country only when they were freed, and that attempting to do it the other way round could result only in superimposing on top of their existing bondage one of a much worse kind, with a country whose record in human rights was appalling.

By accepting, on the simple say-so of Argentina, not only that she had a claim to the islands but that that claim had a greater validity than Britain's own right, and then

proceeding to set in motion the machinery to enable
Argentina to acquire the islands, regardless of islanders'
real needs could only terminate in the way it did, with the
islanders, when they were permitted voice, failing to be
lured by greed of gain to favour Lease Back, so glowingly
presented to them. What they wanted was a gain of a
more basic kind, a right to feel free citizens in their own
land. Opting for a Freeze on negotiations was a first step
in that direction.

A lingering continuation of negotiations was
something the Argentine Government could not permit.
It had a deadline to meet. A quick solution was also
necessary to appease its own people growing restive
under a worsening state of the economy — there had been
street demonstrations. Immediately, to show its
diplomatic displeasure, it refused to publish the
communiqué agreed at the 1982 talks to be made public
three days later in both countries. Then adopting a ploy
which had served it well in the past, it decided to stage an
incident — this time of such impressiveness that it would,
like the 1966 hijack, gain world publicity. Accordingly, a
small naval force was despatched to South Georgia,
ostensibly to help land a team of metal demolition
workers. An Argentine firm had secured from Salvesens
of Edinburgh a contract to strip the metal from their old
whaling station at Leith Harbour.

On landing, the group hoisted the Argentine flag and
refused to go, when told they must, to Grytviken to clear
their documents of entry with the British Administration.
Not discouraged by talks with the British Ambassador in
Buenos Aires, the Argentine Government went further.
Menacing movements of its military ships were reported.
There was an increase in over-flights of Stanley — over-
flying the little town had become a habit Argentina
indulged in whenever she felt displeased. A fortnight after
the landing on South Georgia the Argentine Government
took the ultimate step. What diplomacy had failed to give
it it chose to take. On 2 April, 1982, Argentina invaded
the Falklands.

Index